Follow The Joy:
A Memoir

by

Jason Scott Kurtz

The names of people in the book, besides myself,
have been changed to protect their privacy.

Cover design by Pascale Bridge
Cover illustration by Andy Bridge

Author photo by Michael Benabib

Alan Steinfeld Publishing

ISBN: 0984329226
ISBN-13: 9780984329229
Library of Congress Control Number: 2012954427
CreateSpace Independent Publishing Platform
North Charleston, South Carolina

To my wife

Dayna

Loving you makes me happy

"It is better to live your own destiny imperfectly than to live an imitation of somebody else's life with perfection."

The Bhagavad-Gita

Arrival

I watch, petrified, as the other members of flight 756 open the glass doors and step outside. A roar of noise shatters the serenity of the airport terminal as a screaming mob of Indian men, women and children engulfs them. I try to follow the passengers' progress, but they disappear among shouting voices and sweating bodies.

The doors close softly behind them and tranquility returns to the terminal. Outside, however, countless eyes peer through the glass doors and stare at me, the only foreigner left in the airport. I'm a skinny, t-shirt clad Westerner holding a gigantic green duffel bag tightly in my arms. It offers scant protection from the mob I have to face. I swallow hard, walk towards the doors and step outside.

"Taxi!" a dozen bedraggled Indian men shout, reaching for my bag.

"Money," beg scores of women, motioning with their hands towards their mouths.

"A sweet," dust-covered children cry, looking up at me with hopeful eyes.

I stand among a seething multitude, confused and afraid. Over the heads of the desperate crowd, I see a line of black taxis stretching towards the horizon. Drivers wearing gray, button down, short sleeve shirts lean against the trunks of their cars, watching the chaos with only casual interest. I hold a ticket for one of these taxis in my hand, but I have no idea how to use it.

I search the frantic horde for a friendly face. Amidst the commotion, one man stands still. He meets my gaze, nods, and steps forward with a sense of self-assurance. The crowd parts for him, and he tugs at the ticket in my hand.

Having grown up near New York City, I think I have good instincts about how to protect myself. I know that if I let him take the ticket, I'll have to follow him, so I tighten my grip. The short, stocky man glances at the ticket then snatches my duffle bag from my grasp. I watch, dumbfounded, as he marches down the row of taxis, my luggage dragging behind him on the ground.

I run after him.

As we emerge from the crowd and move past the taxis, the drivers wake from their stupor and shout at my guide, gesturing that he should put my bag in the trunk of their cars. He ignores them, but stops to glance at my ticket once or twice as we go. This helps me hold onto the illusion that this situation is under control and that the ticket I bought, and not this stranger, will determine my fate. When we finally stop, however, reality and panic set in.

I bought a "non-air condition" taxi ticket in the airport terminal. I wanted to travel as local Indians do, not start my trip like a pampered American tourist. I should have reconsidered when the visibly shocked ticket seller explained that an air-conditioned taxi was "more comfortable," but I insisted that a non air-conditioned car was what I wanted. Now, however, I understand the ticket seller's surprise.

The car's body is dented all over, like a very large and very angry man beat it with a sledgehammer. Cracks riddle the windshield beneath a thick coat of lumpy brown slime, in the midst of which two large blurry circles – clearly rubbed away by the sleeve of the driver in a vain attempt to improve visibility – give the impression of frightened eyes. Inside, ripped seats spill clumps of cushioning onto the floor, where the last remaining vestige of carpeting has been worn thin by the footsteps of thousands of people, revealing the cold metal of the car's frame.

It's clear that this car doesn't have air-conditioning. But does it have brakes? I may have been too naïve to pay for air-conditioning, but I would have paid extra for brakes!

I stare in dismay as my guide puts my bag in the trunk. If I want to switch taxis, I'll have to grind through the mob behind me, return to the airport, buy another ticket from the ticket seller, come back outside, push my way through the crowd a third time and try to find my new taxi, this time without the little man's help. I'd also have to remove my bag from the trunk and deal with an angry guide and driver, when I don't speak their language. I take a deep breath, climb into the back seat and close the car door.

The driver gets in the front, turns towards me and takes my ticket. Outside, the man who led me here stares at me. He thrusts his hand through the car's open window, palm up, and says, "baksheesh." My guidebook, which I read on the flight over, explained that "baksheesh" means "tip, donation, or bribe." Since he carried my bag to the taxi, I probably owe him something.

I reach into my pocket and pull out the coins I received at the airport's Currency Exchange Booth. I start to look them over, but the man's brooding presence intimidates me, and I feel that counting the change makes me look cheap, so I simply put them all into his outstretched hand.

He flings the money back at me.

"Baksheesh," he shouts, cupping his hand and shaking it under my face.

Chastised, I reach into my wallet and hand him a 10-rupee bill. He takes it, but furrows his brow in disgust. I give him five more and he starts to yell at me in Hindi. I have a feeling I've already overpaid him, but between his anger and my ignorance I don't know what to do.

My driver saves me. He looks over his shoulder and says something to the guide. The man scowls resentfully, but pockets the money and walks away.

The driver starts the engine, and we slowly head back toward the horde of beggars. They surround the car and stare at me with despondent eyes. Row upon row of bone-thin women and children, desperate and hungry, plead at my window.

It's almost unbearable to look at them and do nothing, but I don't have enough rupees to give something to everyone. I know that if I give money to some, I'll feel even more guilty about the people to whom I give nothing, so I shake my head no as we pass by.

Once we're past the beggars, the driver picks up his pace. He looks at the ticket and then glances back towards me.

"Colaba?" he asks.

"Yes," I reply.

He turns around. We are on our way.

I watch the airport recede behind me, and feel a momentary sense of relief, followed by panic.

"Do you know any good hotels in Colaba?" I ask.

The driver smiles at me in the rear view mirror, but says nothing.

"Do you speak English?"

He shakes his head no, and reality sinks in. I'm on my own. Even if we get to Colaba, which my guidebook said had the cheapest hotels, I have no idea what I'll do when I get there. No one knows where I am, and no one expects to hear from me anytime soon. I remind myself that this is what I wanted. And I remember that this has worked out before. But what if, this time, I don't get out unscathed?

2.

"How could you quit that job?" my mother screamed. I was 23 years old, living at home in New Jersey, and had just quit my entry-level position in a prestigious New York public relations firm. It was the second career I abandoned in the last two years, and my mother was furious.

"I wish we couldn't support you like this," she continued, exasperated. "Then you'd have to find the fortitude to keep working!"

I felt like I'd been punched in the stomach. "You wish I was forced to work in a job I hate?"

"You'll never get anywhere until you find some backbone," was her frustrated reply.

I turned my back on her and stormed away. I refused to accept that I had to work in a job that I hated. My father had always been a miserable, angry person. In college, he had focused on acting, but upon graduation gave up on his dreams and instead joined the family accounting firm. He resented his father's older partners, and as far as I could tell, hated everything about accounting. I didn't know if this had created the unhappy person I knew, but I was sure it was a contributing factor.

If only I knew what I wanted to do! Unlike my father, I wouldn't let anyone stop me. But I didn't know. So I bounced from job to job, hoping that something would click and I'd discover a career that excited me. In the meantime, I lived in my childhood bedroom (not the best way to meet women, or nurture any sense of self esteem). I knew I had to get away from my parents, and out of their house, if I wanted to preserve my belief that I could and would figure things out. Fortunately, my friend Brian offered me an escape.

I had known him since I was four years old. Rumor had it that at 9 months, when normal children began to crawl, he could already run at full speed. It's been that way ever since. If we learned a new game, he mastered it. If we played a sport, he won. Most kids envied him. Some hated him. He made people who were used to excelling feel inferior. I already felt inferior, so this didn't bother me. In fact, he could do no wrong in my eyes. Because he liked me! I lived in fear of the day he'd realize how mediocre I was, but he never did. In fact, he was convinced I could do what he could do. I did my best to accommodate this delusion by being a companion in his adventures.

While in college, we spent a summer month working in London, before traveling throughout Europe. It was one of the best experiences in my life, and I never would have gone without Brian. He made the plans. He set the itinerary. He read the maps and made the arrangements. I simply tagged along. And now, he planned to go to Guatemala for three weeks to brush up on his Spanish – naturally, he spoke fluently already. Since I had quit my job, I asked if I could go with him. As usual, he was happy to have my company.

Even so, this venture was not without risk. Recently, an angry Guatemalan mob had beaten an American backpacker into a coma after a rumor spread that she had abducted a child in order to steal his organs. According to the many reports about this incident, a large number of Guatemalans believed American tourists killed children and harvested their organs, which, it was said, would be sold on the international black market. In response to this tragic incident, the American government issued a travel advisory warning Americans not to visit Guatemala. Under no circumstances were they to travel alone to remote areas of Guatemala. Brian was undeterred. He couldn't fail at anything. I on the other hand…I figured I'd be fine as long as I was with Brian.

We spent two weeks in Antigua, a peaceful town nestled between mountaintops, known for its Spanish language schools. We hired private tutors, studied Spanish, danced the salsa, watched movies, and relaxed. We had planned to spend the last week traveling together, but the day before we were to leave Brian changed his mind.

"What do you mean you want to be alone?" I asked, dumbfounded. "What am I supposed to do?"

"You should visit Lake Atitlan," he replied. "I've been there before, and it's very beautiful. In three days we can meet up in Chichicastenango."

"I can't travel alone," I said. "I don't speak Spanish, remember?"

"You'll be fine," Brian laughed, as if I was joking. "I just need a few days to myself. It's not a big deal. I'll put you on the right bus. All you have to do is find a hotel for one night, take a boat tour, hang out in town for a day, and the next day get a bus to Chichi. You'll be fine."

I tried to persuade him that this was stupid. I only studied Spanish for two weeks! What if a mob accused me of stealing organs? But Brian laughed at me. He was sure I could get by with my rudimentary Spanish. He believed, without hesitation, that I'd be all right.

I was terrified. I was supposed to accompany Brian, who would make sure everything turned out okay. Instead I found myself saying goodbye to Brian as I boarded the bus to Lake Atitlan, thinking, bitterly, that this might be the single most dangerous and stupid thing I had ever done. Guatemalan busses were old, rusted derelicts. Gifts from Russia during the Cold War. In a sane world they would have been sent to a junkyard a decade ago and put out of their misery. To make matters worse, Guatemalan ticket collectors received a percentage of ticket sales, which encouraged them to force as many people inside as possible. The "Getting around" section of my Spanish workbook actually contained the word "duck" because bus drivers sometimes had to ask passengers to hunker down so they could see out the rear view mirror. The most frightening part, however, was that the drivers bounced along the unpaved mountain roads with reckless speed. Front-page newspaper headlines often featured pictures of crumpled busses, which had fallen off the high mountain passes.

The bus to Lake Atitlan, as expected, was rusted, creaky, and crammed full of passengers, many seated next to large, wiry chicken coups. I stood in the aisle, wedged my feet against the seat legs and tried to prepare myself for a four hour, jarring, bone rattling bus ride, when I heard a friendly voice, in English no less, say, "Want to sit down?"

I looked down and was shocked to see a pretty white girl, wearing blue jeans and a gray t-shirt, sitting to my right. Amidst the chaos of the people and the clucking of petrified chickens, I hadn't noticed her.

"Sure," I said. "Thanks." She said something to the people next to her and they scrunched over to make room for me. I sat down and smiled, "I didn't even see you there."

"Yeah. I kind of blend in," she deadpanned. I paused, worried about how incredibly dense I must seem, when I saw her trying to maintain a straight face.

"Yeah. All right." I said. We laughed.

"I'm Jason."

"Marie."

"Nice to meet you." We shook hands. "So," I began, "what's a nice girl like you doing in a place like this?" I had to force myself not to grimace at my own stupid line, but it was the best I could come up with.

"Ha," she said. "I've been here for almost two years, working for the Peace Corps. I'm living in a Mayan village, in the mountains above Lake Atitlan. So, what's a nice guy like you doing in a place like this?"

"Hmm," I exhaled. "Good question. I'm going to Lake Atitlan for a day, and then I'm meeting a friend in Chichi. I'm really just passing time until I meet up with my friend."

"So," she said. "What do you do in your real life?"

"I'm not really sure. I just quit a job working for a public relations firm. It was pretty awful."

"Yeah," she agreed. "Working can suck sometimes. When I get out of the Peace Corps, I think maybe I'll be a teacher. At least that helps people."

"That sounds good," I offered.

"Glad you think so. Ach," she grabbed her head.

"What's wrong?"

"Nothing. I just have a headache. I've been on this bus for six hours. It's almost impossible to relax on these things."

"Yeah, I bet…" I paused. I had an idea. Normally I'd be too shy to speak up, but in this case what did I have to lose? In a couple of hours I'd probably never see her again. "Would you like to try something?" I asked.

"What?"

"Tell me what you like to do? What's relaxing for you?"

"Skiing. I love to ski, but it's been two years since I've had a chance. Any possibility you can get me on a ski slope?"

"Let's see," I replied. "Close your eyes. Go ahead. It's okay. I wouldn't kill you in front of so many witnesses. Take a few deep breaths. Try to relax. Breathe. Imagine you're at your favorite ski slope. Try to see it as clearly as you can. It's a crisp, cool day. There's not a cloud in the sky. It snowed last night, so the course is really fresh. You stand on top of the mountain, looking down. The wind is in your face. Feel the coolness of the wind. Breathe it in. Small snowflakes float in the air, and they feel cool as they touch your cheek. You push off, and you're skiing nice and easy. Everything's flowing by you. You've never felt so free and at ease. Breathe in the cool air. Feel the rhythm of your skis, going side to side. Relax. Easy. Keep going. Breathe…"

I let my voice trail off, and watched her breathe gently. After a few moments, she opened her eyes.

"That was nice." She smiled. "You're interesting. You can visit me at the village sometime if you want."

I felt a rush of excitement at the idea. That would be awesome! But how could I? I spoke virtually no Spanish, and it was dangerous to travel alone. It was especially dangerous to go to small villages.

"Great!" I found myself saying. "I'd love to visit. Maybe I can go with you when we get to Lake Atitlan?"

"No," she said. "I have a friend staying with me right now. But you can come by tomorrow morning if you want."

"Well," I sighed softly. "I'd like to, but how would I get there?"

"You can take a local bus from the Lake. I'll write the name of the town down for you. Just ask the driver and he'll tell you what to do. Come after nine. I'll show you around and we can get breakfast."

"Sounds good," I said, wondering what about dying, alone, in a remote Mayan village sounded good to me.

I wasn't even sure I could manage to get myself a hotel room, but with the help of a handy Spanish phrase book I did. The next morning, though I knew it would be wiser and safer to take a guided tour of the lake, I was so excited at the prospect of visiting Marie that I never considered doing anything else. Instead, I went to the bus depot and showed waiting passengers the name Marie had written down until someone pointed to one of the parked busses. I got on board, we drove up the mountainside, and an hour and a half later the driver stopped the bus and nodded to me. I got off and looked around.

I stood by a small dirt path that climbed over a grassy incline away from the main dirt road. There was no indication that anyone lived nearby and there were no street signs. I decided I was supposed to follow the small path, and walked in that direction. Fifteen minutes later, I was still walking. The path split a few times, and I doggedly continued in the same direction figuring, if I never found the village, at least I could probably make my way back to the main road.

Finally, after almost thirty minutes, I spotted two young boys up ahead. I ran after them, desperate for help.

"Conoces una mujer, Marie?" I said in my awkward Spanish.

They looked at each other, smiled and shrugged their shoulders.

"Una mujer blanca," I said.

"Oh," recognition lit up one boy's face. "La gringa!"

"Si," I replied, thinking that sounded exactly right. "La gringa."

He and his friend ran ahead, laughing. I hurried after them, over hills and streams, until we entered a small town. The boys led me through the back of a bar, where squat, Indian men put their beers down and stared at me, outside past a gurgling brook and finally to the door of a small wooden hut. The boys pointed triumphantly. "La gringa!" they shouted.

I knocked lightly on the door, afraid some large angry man would open it.

Instead, Marie poked her head out.

"La gringa," I said flashing a satisfied grin.

"Is that what he called me?" she said, looking at the boy standing proudly behind me. "Then, I guess that's me. You made it."

"Yeah. I did."

"Come on in. Well, actually…" she looked behind her, "my room's a mess. It's the maid's day off. Let me show you around outside instead."

She led me away from her hut. "This village is very poor and hungry, so I'm raising rabbits," she said, as we walked towards a large rabbit cage. "The idea is that they breed, well, like rabbits, so if the villagers care for them they can be a constant food source. The problem is, they eat all the rabbits at once, without giving them a chance to mate, and then expect me to buy new ones. It's very frustrating, but I try to understand their point of view. Foreigners have been here before, thinking that they know best, and they resent that attitude. I don't blame them for that, but I do think I can help them…I don't know. I've been here for almost two years, and I have no idea if I've done any good at all.

"When I first got here, I tried to blend in. I wanted to live like they did. The person who was here before me hired a local woman to wash her laundry, but I thought I would do it myself. The Mayan women wash their clothes in that stream over there, and I tried to do the same. I totally destroyed a good pair of jeans. Just ripped it to shreds on one of those rocks. When I felt closer to some of the women, I asked how they did it. And they showed me. They put their hand between the clothes and the rock, so the hand takes the abuse and the clothes are unharmed. After that, I just hired one of them to do my laundry for me.

"You know," she continued. "I'm not sure why I'm telling you all this. It's nice that you came, but except for the local bar, there's really nothing to do here besides chores and sleep. Let me take you back into town. I'll buy you breakfast."

I was crushed, but tried to dampen my dismay. I had harbored hopes of a romantic interlude, and even though I knew it was a fantasy, as I was too shy and insecure to initiate anything, it was upsetting that she'd ask me to leave so soon. Still, I kept up my end of small talk as we hitched a ride down the mountain. I let her buy me a roll at a local bakery and tried to offer a friendly smile when she departed.

Despite feeling disappointed that Marie had left, I was ecstatic that I had made it to the Mayan village. The mere fact that I had been able to find the right bus, get off at the right stop, and negotiate the unmarked roads to find the village seemed like a miracle. And I marveled that I had had the courage to take this kind of risk. Somehow the feeling of joy I experienced when I thought about finding Marie overrode my customary reticence, and it was thrilling to discover that I could successfully throw caution to the wind and be spontaneous. For the first time in my life, I felt like Brian was right. Perhaps I didn't have to settle for being mediocre.

3.

Two years later, I quit another job – my parents were obviously thrilled –
and I decided to travel again. The only real happiness I had had in the last
two years came in that moment I deviated from the plan and followed that
feeling of joy to the Mayan village. I wanted to see if I could experience
that again. While in Guatemala, other tourists raved about Costa Rica.
They said it was beautiful and safe. I figured I could blow the money I
saved the last two years, go whitewater rafting, immerse myself in rain
forests, and improve my Spanish at the same time.

There were dozens of language schools in Costa Rica, and I wondered
how to pick the best one. I thought, if only I could visit them, I would
know which one to choose. And then I thought, why can't I visit them first?
After all, I found a remote Mayan village by myself. How hard would it be
to find a school in the capitol city of Costa Rica? And besides, the best part
of my Guatemalan trip was the part which had been spontaneous. Maybe
I could do an entire trip this way?

So I boarded the plane without knowing where I would go when I
arrived. When we landed I took a taxi into the center of town and got a
hotel room. A few days later I enrolled in a three month Spanish language
program and signed up for their home stay package. I was thrilled. Not
in the least because the granddaughter of my new hostess was the runner
up in the previous year's Ms. Costa Rica Pageant. She was stunning –
beautiful, intelligent, talented, and sarcastic. She visited her grandmother
often, which meant I had ample opportunity to secretly moon over her.
Unfortunately, her newest boyfriend – they changed frequently – almost

always accompanied her to our house. They were inevitably young, handsome, talented, and very rich. I could never compete, but she was kind, and introduced me to them as "an American writer" as I was working on a couple of short stories at the time. This seemed impressive, until one of her boyfriends turned out to be a professional poet. "I work on my writing with the Circulo de Poetas," he told me. "Perhaps you have heard of it? It's headed by Laureano Alban, the Costa Rican poet laureate."

I hadn't heard of it, but I was impressed.

"You can come with me sometime, if you want," he said nonchalantly. I realized he was showing off for his girlfriend, and might not really want me to come. I also didn't think my rudimentary Spanish abilities would be sufficient for me to understand what was going on, but I didn't care. I wanted to meet the poet laureate, and I wanted to see what it was like to be part of a professional writing group.

"That sounds amazing," I said. "When can we go?"

He drew his head back, visibly surprised. "Well," he smiled hesitantly, "it's on Thursdays. I'm going this Thursday, of course, but I don't think I'll have time to pick you up. You couldn't find it on your own."

I felt my spirits sag. Many streets in San Jose didn't have names, and most houses didn't have numbers. Directions were often given in relation to known landmarks, none of which I would know.

"Can you give me directions?" I persisted.

"It would be too hard to find," he shook his hand at me, dismissively.

"Come on Carlos," his girlfriend elbowed him playfully in the ribs, "at least tell him how to go."

He looked at her, then shrugged his shoulders. "Sure. It's three blocks north of the old post office, and two blocks west. It's the third house on the right. It's blue, and has a small white fence. I really don't think you could find it on your own, though."

"Hold on," I said. "Let me write this down. You're going this Thursday?"

"Yes."

"OK. Hopefully I'll see you there."

"You know," he interjected, "the post office isn't there anymore. I'm sure you wouldn't be able to find it."

"Is there any way you could pick me up?" I asked.

"I'm not sure. Not this week. Maybe next week."

I didn't know what the urgency was, but I couldn't wait. I headed out that Thursday, did my best to find the spot where the old post office had been, based on my host mother's directions. I then walked three blocks north and two blocks west. Up ahead, I saw a small blue house, exactly as the poet had described. The door was open, and I saw someone walk inside.

I cautiously stuck my head in the open doorway. Inside a few men and women sat around a long rectangular table.

"Is this the Circulo de Poetas?" I asked, using my best Spanish accent.

"Yes," one of the men replied.

"I'm meeting Carlos. He invited me."

"Great. Come in! Sit here," he indicated the seat to his right. "Are you a published writer?"

"No," I admitted, feeling embarrassed.

"Not even in English," he pressed.

"No. I've never been published."

"Are you a writer?"

"I'm working on my writing."

"That's great! We all have to start somewhere," he said. "Here's my book of poetry." He put a thin purple soft cover book in my hands.

"Wow," I flipped through it. "That's great."

"Do you want it?"

"You mean I can have it?" I said, worried that I had not understood him correctly. "I don't want to take it if it's your only copy."

"Don't worry. I have more. Here, let me sign it for you."

I felt stunned and giddy at his warm reception. And, as additional members of the circle arrived – about fifteen in all – my new friend happily introduced me, and several people gave me copies of their books too.

Throughout, I searched for Carlos, worried I wouldn't continue to be welcome without him.

A door slammed shut behind me. I turned around, and a large, fat man, wearing a rumpled suit and tie approached the table. He had a confident and palpable presence, which insisted on our collective attention. This, I thought, must be Laureano Alban, the poet laureate.

He walked around the table and sat down directly across from me, but didn't look at me.

"Who is this?" he asked the table in general.

"This is a friend of Carlos's," the man to my left replied.

Laureano nodded his head.

"Is Carlos coming today?" he asked.

People looked at me.

"He said he would meet me here," I offered.

Laureano nodded his head again, but said nothing.

He lit a candle, placed it on the table, and reached behind him to turn on a small radio, which played soft music.

"Before we get to today's business," he said in a deep voice, "I have a poem to read."

People sat up in their seats, and their eyes widened. I could feel excitement in the air. I stared at him and concentrated with all my might as he read his poem, but it was beyond my Spanish language abilities.

"Vote," he said when he was finished.

Around the table, people put their hands out. Most of the group gave the thumbs up sign, but two people had their thumbs in a horizontal position. Laureano immediately focused on them.

"What didn't you like?" he demanded.

"Well," one began. "I liked it very much. I just thought it was a little too sentimental in the middle."

"And you," he pointed at the other person. "What didn't you like?"

Again, she liked the poem, but had a minor reservation.

Laureano listened intently, and when the critiques were complete, he began to rip up the poem.

"What are you doing?" people exclaimed. "Don't do that!"

"No," he said, tearing it to shreds. "Laureano Alban does not write mediocre poetry. He only writes great poetry."

He then held the pieces in the candle's flame, letting them burn.

"It was beautiful!" one of the women exclaimed. "Don't do that."

"That's it," he said, dropping the burning pages in a dish. "Let's move on."

With that, he pulled out a large yellow notepad and ran his finger down a list. "Let's talk about some of last week's questions. No, I don't like that one. That's obvious, who wrote that? Oh, here's a good one. What gives poetry its soul?"

I paused to contemplate the question. I loved reading good poetry, but I never considered what made it so moving to me. After a few moments, however, I thought I had an answer. And I thought it was pretty good. I wanted to volunteer, but I hesitated. What if Laureano didn't like it? What if I couldn't articulate my idea in Spanish? Was I supposed to say something? Or, as a guest, without even the guy who invited me here, should I remain silent?

"Poetry has a thousand souls," one woman opined. "It comes from everywhere that life exists. It encompasses everything that is alive"

"Poetry has an eternal soul," another person responded. "It taps into something that is beyond our understanding."

Laureano shook his head, unhappy with what he heard. I was concentrating with all of my might, struggling simply to understand what was being said, when I realized the group had stopped talking. I looked around, and saw the entire table staring at me. Laureano must have asked for my opinion.

I swallowed hard, and began. "Well…I think the soul of poetry has two parts. I think that the first part of a poem's soul comes from the author. He pours his heart and soul into his writing, trying with all his might to use the right words to express his feelings. But the words are only symbols, they are not the real feeling or idea. At best, the poem is a window, through which we can see something that is real. So the right words, alone, are not enough to give poetry its' soul. The second part of a poem's soul comes from the reader. He pours his heart and soul into trying to understand the symbolic language of the poem and to be open to its power and meaning. If he is successful, and if the writer is skilled, then the reader can use the poem's words to open a window within himself to the poet's feelings and ideas, so that he can experience what the writer wanted to express. It's the work of the reader, combined with the work of the writer, that gives a poem its' power and gives a poem its' soul."

As I stumbled along in my broken Spanish, Laureano reached behind him and turned down the music. The table hushed, and I became increasingly nervous. Was I making sense?

Laureano slammed his fist down onto the table. I jumped back in my seat. The candle rocked and flickered, but remained upright.

"That's it!" he exclaimed. "That's right! Did we need an American to come here and teach us about poetry?" He looked around the room, and started teasing people. "What was that stuff about a thousand souls? What were you saying about an eternal soul? Can you believe we needed an American to explain this to us?"

He thrust out his hand, and I shook it.

"You're welcome here anytime!" he said. "I'm glad Carlos invited you. We meet every Thursday. Please come again."

And so I did. Even though it was impossible for me to fully understand the poetry and short stories that people read, it was a thrill for me to be a part of a prestigious writing group. I loved the camaraderie of the writers, and I basked in the idea that I was one of them.

When I left Costa Rica three months later, the Circle of Poets had been the most important part of my trip. I was grateful to myself for having had the courage to follow that inner sense of excitement and find that little blue house. And I wondered why this kind of experience, where unexpected miracles happen, never occurred in my "real" life. And I wondered if they ever would.

4.

When I completed my Master's degree in English Literature in 1997, and I again found myself at a loss about what to do with my life, I began to freak out. I loved reading literature, and I had enjoyed studying for my BA. In the back of my mind, I always thought that if all else failed I could go back to school and become an English Literature professor. So, at the age of 26, I gave up on the idea that I'd find something better and enrolled in a prestigious MA/PHD program. By the end of the first two years, after qualifying for my MA, I realized it was a mistake. Students wouldn't discuss what we were reading in class because they were afraid someone would steal their "brilliant" ideas. Professors were interested only in publishing, and were often so contemptuous of students that they didn't even read our papers. Even more depressing was discovering that one of my favorite professors had to leave the school because he hadn't published anything prestigious enough to warrant them giving him tenure, and without tenure he had no security. This "publish or perish" world did not appeal to me. I didn't want to spend my life struggling to keep myself "relevant," and I didn't want to be in a world where I had to worry that my colleagues were out to steal my ideas.

Which meant I was totally screwed. I was single, lonely, largely broke, with no career and no vision at all for my future. I didn't even have a backup plan anymore. My only options seemed to be to live at home forever, or embark on a professional career track and accept that work would be unpleasant and unfulfilling, which was the very thing I'd spent my adult life avoiding. I practically devoured the self-help and spirituality sections of the bookstore, frantically searching for something that would free me from having to spend my life toiling at a job that didn't make me happy, desperately hoping for a way to avoid following in my father's footsteps.

And something strange happened. It began when I read a collection of stories about an Indian guru named Neem Karoli Baba. He was a completely unpredictable character who, according to the book, knew exactly what to do or say to help his followers find what they were looking for in life, be it love, success, or spiritual growth. The stories didn't make rational sense – he knew their innermost thoughts, and could repeat back to them words they had said only to themselves – but as I read I felt a deep sense of longing. I imagined India to be full of saints and gurus like this man. Perhaps, if I met someone like him, I could unlock the secret to my own happiness.

It was a laughable fantasy. I could never imagine myself massaging the feet of a large fat man, which was how disciples in the book received the guru's blessing, but for some reason I couldn't shake this desire. I didn't know why. I'd never wanted to go to India before. The guru I read about was long dead. But the idea kept popping into my mind. I tried to ignore it. I tried to force myself to forget it, but I kept thinking about India. And whenever I did, I felt happy.

I had recently seen a video of a Franciscan Priest who lectured on the relationship of the mind to God. "The mind is like an old television set," he had said, "where the screen is filled with what we call white noise. Now, many people believe that white noise occurs when the television can't get a clear signal, but this is incorrect. In fact," he continued, "white noise occurs when the television receives too many signals at one time and can't differentiate between them.

"This," he tapped the side of his head, "is like our minds. We have so many voices screaming in our heads that it feels like God is not speaking to us. In fact, God is always trying to communicate with us, but his voice is drowned out by the competing noise – the voices of fear and longing and envy and anger and sadness. It's because of the static of these other voices that we feel that God does not speak to us, but if we can learn to quiet our minds, we will find that we can hear the voice of God quite clearly."

I wondered if this feeling, this call to India, was what he'd been talking about. Could it be that this voice, which whispered of India, knew something I did not know? I had followed a similar feeling in Guatemala and Costa Rica, and my experiences had been more exciting and fulfilling than I anything I could have planned. I realized that if I wanted to figure out how to have meaning in my life, I'd need help. Following this call seemed like my only, and last, hope.

So, I'd travel to India. I'd begin with a meditation retreat to help quiet my mind, but other than that, I'd make no plans at all. I'd follow the call of this voice and see where it led. And I wouldn't come home until I knew what I wanted to do with my life.

5.

Which is how, at 5:00 AM on a Monday morning, I find myself bouncing in the back seat of a non air-conditioned taxi, desperately trying to calm the fear that threatens to make me pee my pants. This seemed like a much better idea when I contemplated it from the safety of New Jersey!

Innumerable potholes scar the roads, as if someone dropped small grenades everywhere. Even though the car has brakes (thank God for that!), the driver would rather turn the wheel viciously and bounce over the potholes than use them. Fortunately, there are few cars on the road. Although he drives recklessly, we do not appear to be in imminent danger. Besides, I tell myself, he's a professional. He must know what he's doing.

As we race along, dust and dirt from the road blow in my face through the car's open windows, but even at this early hour it's too hot to close them. Forget idealism. Next time, if given the choice, I'll hire an air-conditioned car!

This continues, painfully, monotonously, until, after two hours, a terrifying thought seeps into my consciousness. Can Bombay International Airport be this far from Colaba, which, after all, is in Bombay?

"Colaba?" I repeat, nervously.

The driver nods his head, and continues to drive. I take a deep breath and take stock of my situation. I'm sitting in a taxi driven by a man I can't communicate with, traveling through a country I've never been to, heading to a destination I know nothing about. What, exactly, made me think this was a good idea?

After another anxiety filled 30 minutes, my driver slows down, gestures out the window and says something in Hindi. My fear lifts as I realize that we have arrived in Colaba and the driver wants to know which hotel I want to go to.

"The Salvation Army," I say relieved.

He shakes his head and pulls over. I repeat the name, show him the guidebook map, and point at the dot which represents the Salvation Army. He takes the map and looks at it intently, then hands it back and shakes his head again.

I decide to try to pronounce the name of the street the hotel is on. I know that this is a desperate act, as there is almost no chance I can pronounce the Hindi adequately, but what else can I do?

"Mereweather Road," I say.

He shakes his head yet again and calls out to someone by the side of the road. A man walks over and, after a brief conversation with the driver, turns his attention towards me.

"Salvation Army Hostel," I say. "Mereweather Road."

Now both men smile at me and shake their heads. I get desperate and start reading street names from the book in the hopes that I'll say one they recognize.

"P.J. Ramchandani Marg."
"Shahid Bhagat Singh Marg."
"Mahakavi Bhusha Marg."
"Nawroji F. Road."
"Shivaji Marg."
"Best Marg."

One of these names sparks something. The men erupt into a flurry of conversation and suddenly we're off again.

After a few twists and turns I spot a street sign that reads, "Best Marg," and I shout, "Stop!" The guidebook indicates that there are three hotels on this road, and I figure I can get lodging in one of them. I'm excited just to know where I am on the map, and I finally feel like I have some control over my situation.

The driver pulls over, puts the car in park, turns around and looks at me with a serious face.

"Baksheesh," he says.

Somehow I knew he was going to say that.

"Okay," I tell him, "but I want to get my bag out of the trunk first."

I open the door and the driver follows me towards the rear of the car and repeats, "baksheesh."

"Yes," I point to the trunk. "After I get my bag."

He looks at me distrustfully, but opens the trunk and allows me to remove my large, green duffle bag. It's a relief to have my belongings in my arms. No matter what happens now, at least I haven't lost my stuff.

The driver looms over me, nervously waiting for his "baksheesh." I know that having paid for the trip in advance I probably don't really owe him anything, but I feel too insecure to argue with him. I hand the driver a 50-rupee bill, which amounts to a little over a dollar tip, and he pockets the money with a grin so wide that I'm certain I've just been ripped off. It pisses me off to know I've been taken advantage of, but I reassure myself that at least I made it to some place I can name.

My duffle bag covers a large black camping backpack, which contains all my stuff. I remove the backpack from the duffel bag, heave it onto my back, and stagger under its weight. I tried it on at home and I didn't think it was this heavy. Granted, I stuffed it with everything I thought I might need for every possible contingency I could think of – two person tent (in case I make a friend), hiking boots, water purifier, malaria pills, a large metal padlock (I heard that many hotel doors are locked with padlocks and it's safer to have your own), a bathing suit, a winter coat, several warm sweaters, a dozen pairs of socks, twelve tee shirts, a bottle of liquid soap, a cool high tech travel towel (it can hold up to 5x its weight in water!), a meditation bench, and as much underwear as I could pack (if nothing else, I always want at least one clean pair). I pitch myself forward and find that once I get my momentum going, I can stumble along. I feel a moment of despair when I realize that I've consigned myself to travel the subcontinent with this load on my back, but I'll have to worry about that later. For now, I have to find a hotel.

Luck is with me. I find the Hotel Moti International without any trouble. Trees surround the white mansion, and thick patches of green ivy cling to its walls. A large, ornate white gate stands open, revealing a long driveway which runs next to the house. The building, once majestic, now sags under the weight of its years. The white paint is cracked and peeling. The windows are cracked and dirty. The ivy hangs down like a tangled, unwashed head of hair.

"Do you have any rooms?" I ask the man sitting on the hotel's stairs.

He nods his head and I follow him inside, trying not to tip over backwards as I climb up the stairs. We enter a dimly lit vestibule, where the man walks behind a large counter, retrieves a key and heads down the narrow hallway. He unlocks the last door on the left and I step inside. The room has 10-foot-high ceilings, a ceiling fan (Indian air conditioning), and a king size bed with a visibly lumpy mattress. The bed and a chest of drawers almost fill the room to capacity, and I have to squeeze between them to get to the bathroom, which has a toilet and a showerhead but no shower. The showerhead simply sticks out from the wall next to the toilet. Everything is faded and run down, just like the building, but it's spacious, "air-conditioned" and has a bathroom.

"How much?" I ask, expecting the price in my guidebook of 550 rupees to be correct.

"800 rupees," he replies.

I look at him with a strained smile. He's testing me, isn't he?

"I thought it would be 550."

He smiles at me and shrugs his shoulders. "800 rupees," he repeats.

Fear and anger percolate in me. I was originally hoping to pay 100 rupees for a bed at the Salvation Army. Out of desperation, I decided I would splurge and pay 550. Now, if I want to avoid lugging my 1,000-pound backpack around Colaba I'll have to pay 800 rupees. I'll have gone from

$2.50 to $20. To make matters worse, I hoped to limit my expenses to $30 per day. If I take this room I'll have spent almost $30 in my first 3 hours.

I quickly come up with a few rationalizations to help me swallow this bitter pill. It's 7:30 AM and I already feel as if I've had a long day. It's my first day in India and I ought to treat myself. Twenty dollars is a small price to pay to avoid getting a hernia lugging my overweight backpack all over India.

"I'll take it." I say feeling depressed and defeated.

I hadn't anticipated this, but I'm suddenly very concerned about overpaying. In a foreign country where I don't speak the language and don't know what I'm going to do, my only sense of empowerment comes from the fact that I have 3,000 American dollars, which I know is a fortune here. Though I came to India hoping to relinquish control and let life and my instincts guide me, actually doing so terrifies me. Each time I overpay for a service, I feel like a man drifting out into an unknown sea, getting further and further away from his one sense of stability, a rapidly disappearing shore, which is somehow connected to the size of his wallet.

The man smiles at me and takes me back to the counter. I sign my name and country of origin in a register and pay him the exorbitant fee. I then drag my bag down the hallway and into my room, lock the door behind me and lie down on the bed. As soon as my guard is down, the stress of being in a strange place, feeling exposed, alone, and helpless overwhelms me. Within moments, I fall asleep.

6.

I wake up feeling somewhat refreshed and surprisingly dirty. The air in my room is thick with dust. The ceiling fan, while keeping me cool, has the unpleasant side effect of moving the dust around the room, which makes me want to sneeze. In addition, my skin has a greasy feeling now and I wonder if these sheets are clean. I quickly stop wondering when I realize I don't really want to know.

I rub my eyes and take stock of my situation. When I embarked on this trip, I intentionally avoided an agenda or predetermined goals which I thought might get in the way of listening to that ephemeral voice which had guided me in Guatemala and Costa Rica. My one acquiescence to rational planning was to sign up for a meditation course that would begin tomorrow afternoon. I figured this would help quiet the din of my overactive mind, help me be more aware of my inner guide, and put me in position to meet people who could suggest places to go and things to do.

Consequently, what I really need to do today is purchase a train ticket to the town of Igatpurri, where the meditation center is located. Unfortunately, I have no idea where Igatpurri is, how long the train will take, or what will happen when I get there. When I pick up my guidebook to try to figure this out, my hand shakes slightly, and I can feel my heart beating fast.

What *am* I doing in India? Am I, as my parents intimated, running away from the difficult choices of adult responsibility, or is it really possible that taking the stereotypical Indian "spiritual" journey will awaken me to a fulfilling future? It would be humiliating to return home, after all the drama of packing my bags and leaving the country, to find that I am no different than I was before.

I steady my hand and open the guidebook. Mumbai, which is the Indian name for Bombay, has five different train stations: Victoria, Dadar, Churchgate, Kurla, and Mumbai Central. They are all distinct rail lines, each going to different destinations. I have a vague idea that Igatpurri is north of Bombay and my guidebook says Mumbai Central has trains going north. Should I: A) ask someone for directions; B) assume that Mumbai Central has the train I want; or C) curl up in a ball on the bed and cry. Since I'm an American man, I'm not going to choose A or C, which leaves me with B, go to Mumbai Central and hope for the best.

I leave the hotel and head towards a taxi that I see parked on the side of the street. As I approach it, a bundle of rags, heaped on the sidewalk, slowly unfurls, stands up, and turns into a tall, skinny woman.

"Give Babu," she shouts, shuffling forward and waving a bandaged hand in my direction.

Her face is pot marked and scarred and her hand, cupped slightly, seems to have been burned in a fire where all her fingers melted together.

I realize it's leprosy and it terrifies me. Is it contagious? I back away until I bump into the taxi.

"Give Babu," she shouts again, closer now.

I open the car door and shut it behind me. Still, she approaches.

I make a concerted effort to look in her eyes while I shake my head no. I want to acknowledge her as a human being, but I had heard that the mafia controls beggars in India and I decided before I came I wouldn't support organized crime.

"Food, Babu," she says. "Give," she insists.

"No," I say. "I'm sorry."

I turn towards the driver. "Mumbai Central." I say.

"Forty rupees sir," he says.

Forty rupees sounds like a lot for what I assume is a short ride, but the leper woman is approaching. "Fine. Let's go."

I slouch in the car, hoping that the engine will start and the car will pull away before the woman reaches my window. Nothing happens, and suddenly she thrusts her diseased hand into the car.

"Give babu!" she shouts.

I press myself against the other side of the car.

"I'm sorry," I say.

"Give!" She stares at me, waving her disfigured hand at me, gesturing at her decaying mouth.

What's the driver waiting for? I tap him on the shoulder.

"Ready?" I ask him.

He looks at me, then nods and turns the ignition key.

The woman gets agitated and begins to yell at me and gesture more and more violently with her stubby hand.

"Give. Give. Give," she shouts angrily.

I turn again and look her in the eyes and say, "No. I'm sorry."

We pull away, and the woman spits on the ground and curses me. The hatred in her voice chills me.

I hate confrontations. Even though I'm an adult, capable of leaping into the unknown third world, I feel terrified when someone gets angry at me. It's a relief to leave the leper behind.

We arrive at the station. I pay the driver and enter. The hallways swarm with countless people who knock into me and push me aside as I wander about. I don't know where I'm going. I don't see any employees and all the signs are in Hindi.

I wander blindly through the hallways and into many crowded rooms until I discover a large room where there is a window which, in English, says "Enquiry." In front of the window, a small group of people fights for position, bracing their feet against the floor for leverage, pushing and squeezing past and between each other in a desperate battle to get to the front. Surprisingly, despite the intense struggle going on, people don't look at each other and they don't say anything. They simply try to muscle their way through.

I stand in the back of the crowd, hoping I can politely wait my turn. It's silly, considering the primitive struggle taking place in front of me, but I'm accustomed to waiting and some desperate part of my brain hopes that people will see me standing here and respect my act of courtesy.

Unfortunately, when new people arrive they push past me and thrust themselves into the group. After 15 minutes I'm no closer to the front and the mass of people has grown larger. I feel like each person who ignores me and moves in front of me is effectively giving me the finger. I stifle my anger until I can't take it anymore.

I thrust myself forward and soon am part of the mob, hemmed in on all sides. It's hard to breathe and it's a struggle to stand my ground. When someone reaches the window, the struggle ceases momentarily, and when that person finishes and tries to depart, the group makes way for the man to leave. But as soon as he has passed, a quiet fight ensues as we all strive to make it to the front. In India I have a slight height advantage, even though I'm only 5' 7". Also, I'm young, healthy and fit, so once my frustration has overwhelmed my civilized demeanor and I'm willing to push and slice my way between people, I make good progress. After the man behind the counter helps a few people he notices me – my short brown hair, green eyes, and white skin stick out in this crowd – and he motions for me to come to the front. The people around me reluctantly move aside, and instantly press forward in my wake to try to establish a better position, literally pushing me into the window.

"I need to buy a ticket to Igatpurri," I tell the man, panting slightly from my effort.

He shakes his head sadly and despair begins to creep into my stomach.

"There are no trains to Igatpurri from here?" I ask.

He shakes his head again.

"Where can I get one?"

"Victoria Station."

"Do I have to buy the ticket there?" I ask in desperation. The last thing I want to do is go to another train station and fight through another crowd.

"Yes," he replies.

"What time does the train leave?"

"Any time."

"Can I buy the ticket in the morning?"

"Yes."

I turn around, the crowd parts for me, and I leave feeling defeated and dejected. How am I going to survive here if trying to buy a train ticket intimidates and exhausts me?

I exit the station, hoping to walk a bit and clear my head, but the sidewalk is overrun with street who thrust things into my hands, or grab my arms and pull me towards their stores.

"Here, sahib, buy this."

"This will look good on you, baba."

"Good price. Come see. Good price."

I literally have to pull my hands out of their grasp and ball up my fists as they attempt to put things in my hands. I try to keep moving, hoping this will prevent them from grabbing me, but it only results in the store owners trying to block my passage with their bodies. I walk faster and faster until I'm cruising along the sidewalk, walking as fast as I can, not daring to pause long enough in front of a store to identify what they sell for fear that the proprietor will stop me and insist that I buy something.

A flash of red catches my attention. Across the street is a cute little Indian girl, maybe six years old, wearing a bright red dress. She stares intently at me, crosses the street, walks up to me, grabs my pinkie, and smiles.

It's flattering to have my kind and gentle nature recognized amidst all of these people. Suddenly, the salesmen's pressure vanishes.

"Hello," I say sweetly, flashing my most endearing smile.

"Hi," she replies, smiling back at me. "What's your name?"

"Jason," I say slowly, careful to enunciate it so she will understand.

She pulls my finger, and we start to walk.

"My name is Jana," she says. "Where are you from?"

"America."

"I'm from India."

I laugh. Her innocence is delightful.

"I thought so," I reply.

She pulls my finger again, and we stop walking.

"Will you buy me some milk?"

I look up to see that we've stopped in front of a street vendor. Without being asked, the man behind the counter pulls out a box of milk powder the size of an American economy box of detergent. The man tells me that the price is "400 rupees."

I realize I've been had.

I was warned about this scam by a friend back at home. He told me that it was common for Indian children to ask foreigners to buy them powdered milk for their starving families. The scam is that store owners have pre-arranged deals with the children. The child convinces the foreigner to buy the milk, and when the foreigner walks away the child goes back to the store and returns the box of milk for some money. The foreigner goes home convinced he or she has fed a starving family; the girl and the storeowner get paid. It's a perfect scam where everyone walks away happy.

"If you meet a child that you really feel sorry for and you want to buy her some milk, then make sure you open the box so it can't be re-sold," my friend warned me. "In this way, the child's family will have to drink the milk. Otherwise, you are just contributing to a very old con."

I look down at the little girl, embarrassed to have been so easily led.

"No. I'm sorry. I can't buy you that."

The large box is instantly replaced with a smaller container. This one costs 200 rupees.

It's a sad sign of what an easy mark I am, that despite my knowledge of the scam, I consider buying the smaller box and ripping it open. But then I realize that the girl is wearing a new dress, and I don't really know if she needs the milk or not.

I say no again, turn away from the vendor, and try to walk away. The little girl starts pulling on my pinkie with all her might.

"Please!" She screams. "Pleeeeease!"

I yank my hand from her grasp. "Sorry. No."

She grabs my other hand and tries to pull me back to the store. "Some sweets!"

Again, I consider the request. Again, I refuse.

I try to walk away, but she holds onto my finger, and leans her body towards the stand with all her strength.

"Some rupees," she says with a sob. Now she's crying.

And I break. I can't let her cry. I pull out a 10-rupee coin and hand it to her. The tears vanish. She smiles, grabs the coin, and runs away. I feel mixed emotions as I watch her go. It only took 10 rupees to satisfy her, but was I right to allow a scam to pay off?

I move forward again only to discover that another girl, this time wearing a pretty white dress, is watching me. By the look in her eyes I can tell she saw the entire episode. She heads straight towards me, and before I can react, she's holding my pinkie.

"Hello," she says sweetly.

I look around, desperate for some way to avoid this.

"Hello," she repeats.

"Uh. Hello."

"What's your name?"

I want to tell her that I've been through this before, but I can't bring myself to be rude to a child.

"Jason."

"I'm Tihara. Where are you from?"

"America." How do I get out of this?

"I'm from Bombay."

There's no other option. I ignore her and start to walk away.

She tightens her grip on my hand.

"Buy me some milk," she says, trying to pull me over towards another street vendor.

I yank my hand out of her grasp and say, "Sorry, no."

She tries to grab my hand again, but I evade her.

"Some sweets?"

"No."

I turn away from her and start walking down the street, hoping she will just give up and go away.

She doesn't. We walk down the street together, and she repeatedly tries to grab my hand. I jerk away, trying to elude her, while simultaneously trying to ignore her. This soon grows very irritating, and I'm desperate to find someplace where she can't follow me.

I spot a bookseller's shop and pause in front of the display. The vendor motions to the little girl, and she disappears. I breathe a sigh of relief.

As I stand here, collecting myself, I begin to understand just how well organized things are here. There are rules. The little girl is not allowed to interfere with the bookseller's sale. As long as I stand here, I'll be left alone.

I take my time. Books have always provided me with a sense of respite from life's turmoil and browsing eases my tensions. I peruse the rack of books, with great pleasure, relaxing with each title I take in. After I make my purchase and walk away, however, the white angel reappears.

"Sir. Please buy me some milk."

I move past her, but she refuses to be ignored.

"Sir, please buy me some milk. Sir, please buy me some milk. Sir, please buy me some milk."

She repeats this over and over again as I walk down the street, her child's voice easily heard despite the noise of the crowded street.

"Look," I finally say. "I can't buy you any milk."

"Some sweets?"

"No."

"Please give me some rupees."

"No."

"Please buy me some milk."

I give up being reasonable and walk away again, determined to ignore her.

She persists and persists before finally asking, in desperation, "Why not?"

And I wonder: why not? OK, it's a scam. And, yes, I'm being ripped off. But, if I give her 10 rupees she'll go away happy and I won't have to feel like a heel for being stubborn and mean to a little girl. Despite her new dress, she must be poor to be begging on the street. Maybe the money will help her.

But why should I feel guilty for refusing to fall for a scam? Why should the fact that the girl is cute be enough to override my reason? Why should I even have to explain my actions? I don't owe this girl money or explanations. Do I?

"Because I said so," I say, experiencing a moment of guilt and pleasure as I remember all the times my father explained his rejection of my requests this way.

I should have known better. That answer never satisfied me as a child, and it doesn't satisfy her either.

She follows me down the street, repeatedly asking "why" every second or so. If we've walked too many blocks without my responding she starts pleading, "Sir…sir…sir…" so pitifully that I am forced to look at her. Then the litany of requests resumes. "Sir, please buy me some milk. Please buy me some sweets…"

Eventually she deviates from her script and says, "But you gave her some." And I almost lose my resolve. This is the reason for her Herculean persistence. In this moment she is no longer a little scam artist but a little girl, wanting to know why she is different from another girl. My heart begins to break and I'm about to give her a coin when fear makes me reconsider. What if there's another girl watching us? One with a blue dress.

I kneel down and look her in the eyes.

"I'm sorry," I say. "But I gave your friend all the money I'm going to give anybody."

Tears well up in her little brown eyes. I feel like the world's biggest ass, and when she turns and runs away from me I want to cry too.

I race back to my room, close and lock the door, and flop down onto my lumpy bed. I open my book and read, transporting myself away from this unbearable reality, just as I did when I was a child. And I wonder if I'll ever stop feeling like the little kid who can't get anything right.

7.

I wake in the morning, surrounded by the dusty sunshine that fills my room. Yesterday was so painful and overwhelming, it feels like an accomplishment to simply have survived a full day. Every muscle in my body is tight. It literally hurts to get out of bed. All I have to do, I remind myself, is make it to the meditation center. If I do, my trip won't be a complete failure, and hopefully I'll sink into the quiet of meditation and regroup. Otherwise, I'm not sure how long I'll be able to tolerate feeling this helpless.

I pack my bags, and by 10:00 AM I'm ready to go. I hail a taxi driver who offers to take me to Victoria Station for 40 rupees, which sounds like a fair price.

As we drive north, the gigantic red fortress looms over us. Like many relics from the old British Empire, Victoria Station lies in a state of magnificent disrepair. Cracked and peeling gargoyles stare down from their lofty perches. Tall, stout towers loom over the city, in desperate need of a wash. The lions posted at the ancient gates look tired and warn. The gates themselves, rusted and brown, bar entry to none.

But the life surrounding the ancient station hums with vibrant energy. A large, golden McDonalds arch mocks the run down relic from across the street. Billboards, like an army of protesters, surround the station, advertising American brand sneakers and Japanese electronics. A hundred street vendors sell fruit and assorted trinkets from posts along the sidewalk. Cars jam the roads and pedestrians jostle for room to move. As we pull up I notice one especially large and disturbing billboard. It depicts a young woman wearing a short skirt, bending over with her butt sticking out. The caption reads "Monika Lewdinsky." I can't figure out what it advertises, but as an American I'm embarrassed.

I pay the driver and walk into the station. The sheer size of it awes me. The ceilings look 30-feet high and the cavernous rooms swarm with noise and people. I may not know where I'm going, but I do know enough to search for an Enquiry window. When I find one, however, I feel sick. An unorganized and impatient crowd, about fifteen people thick, pushes and strains toward the single window. Like before, I have no choice. I thrust myself into the group and soon struggle and sweat with all the rest. After ten minutes I'm far enough forward for the man behind the window to see me. There's a collective groan when he motions me forward, but people make room.

"I'd like to purchase a ticket to Igatpurri," I say, trying to get my panting under control.

The man shakes his head no, sadly, as if he's sorry he can't help me.

"I was told that there were trains from this station to Igatpurri all the time."

Another negative shake of his head. "Dadar Station," he says.

My stomach feels cold. Dadar Station is far to the North from here.

"Do I have to buy the ticket there?" I ask.

"Yes."

"When is the next train?"

"3:00."

I'm in trouble. I'm supposed to be at the center by 5:00.

"How long does the train take?"

"3 hours."

I'm in big trouble. Although I confirmed my attendance for this course before I left America, I have no idea what will happen if I don't show up by the deadline.

I walk out of the station in a daze.

A policeman oversees an endless line of taxis, which idle alongside the station. I approach him and ask, "Dadar Station?"

He nods and I put my bag in the trunk of the first cab. I get in and we're off.

8.

The meter scrolls up remarkably slowly, one tenth of a rupee at a time. As I watch it, I feel better. At least this will be a cheap ride.

"Chowpatty Beach," the driver says.

Off to my left I can see that we are passing a beach. My memory of the guidebook map was that the coastline is to the west, while the train station is to the north.

"Nehru Park," the driver says, pointing out the window.

Is he giving me a tour of Bombay? I pull out my guidebook and check the map. We're going in the wrong direction.

I tap the driver on the shoulder. "Dadar Station," I say.

He nods his head. "Walkeshwar Temple."

"No. I don't care. I don't want a tour. Just take me to Dadar Station."

He nods his head and points, "Hanging Gardens."

I groan out loud. "Dadar Station," I plead.

"Mahalaxmi Racecourse."

I hate this place.

We arrive at Dadar Station an hour later. I pay the driver, go to the back of the car and open the trunk to retrieve my duffel bag, all the while eyeing the train station, which is on the other side of a busy four-lane highway. There is no crosswalk and I wonder how I'm going to cross the street without getting run over. As I bend over to pick up my bag, I notice a young man, about 18-years-old, watching me intently from across the street. He meets my gaze, then sprints into the street, dodging between speeding cars in his haste to cross. I'm shocked by his recklessness, but the truly strange thing is that he appears to be headed right towards me.

Before I know it he's trying to pull my bag from my hands.

"No thanks," I say, startled. "I can do it."

"Please sir, let me," he insists.

"No thanks," I repeat.

But he won't let go. We engage in a silent struggle for a few moments before I manage to wrest my bag from his grasp.

He lunges for it again and I pull it away from him. He tries again, and again I have to dodge him. I put the bag on my right side, and heave it up on my shoulder, keeping my left side between him and the bag, and I begin to cross the street. There is no crosswalk and no streetlight, so I have to run across the highway and dodge between speeding cars. This would have been tricky if I was unencumbered. It would have been dangerous if I only had to cross while handling my heavy bag. But I find myself dodging cars, while simultaneously pulling my duffel bag away from this man, who despite the danger to us both, continues to try to take my bag from me even as we evade traffic. When I make it to the other side, I turn on the young man in a rage, but he speaks before I do.

"Give me fifty rupees," he demands.

"What? What for?"

"For crossing with you."

"You must be crazy!" I shout at him. "I refused your help. You tried to take my bag from me. You chased me across the street. And you think I'm going to pay you?"

He ignores my question (it was rhetorical anyway) and tries a different tact.

"Which train do you want?" he asks.

At least he's not subtle. If he can't carry my bag for me, he'll earn money by directing me to the correct train.

"Never mind," I say crossly.

"Sir, which train," he says in an exasperated, trying-to-be-patient-with-a-child voice that makes me want to punch him in the face.

I switch tactics. Speaking to this guy is fruitless. Maybe ignoring him will work. I turn away from him and look around. Small stalls which sell the various fruits, spices, and trinkets that seem to be common here bracket the train tracks like parentheses. And there, off in the distance, to my left, I spot the Enquiry window.

"Don't worry about it," I mutter.

"Sir," he sighs. "You need my help. Which train do you want?"

"I'm fine," I say as I walk away, "I know what I'm doing."

Again the young man lunges for my bag, but I pull it away. He follows behind me, alternatively demanding money and insisting that I tell him which train I want. I try to ignore him, but his shouting draws a crowd and we're soon surrounded. I put my bag down and look for a way past these people. The young man says something in Hindi and people in the crowd laugh. He smiles at me, as if I were a rat caught in his trap.

"Give me some money."

"No way."

"Which train do you want?"

"Never mind."

"Sir," he says, arms akimbo, "You'll never find your train without my help. You have to tell me which train." He shouts something in Hindi and again people laugh.

"Look," I say, trying to be reasonable. "Can't you just leave me alone?"

"I can do anything I want," he says smugly.

"That's true," I agree, "but even if you follow me around all day, you won't get a single rupee."

Several people in the crowd laugh, and they translate my remarks. Others laugh and point, watching us with an evil glint in their eyes. We've become entertainment, where the victor may not matter as much as the excitement of the conflict.

The laughter convinces the young man that the crowd isn't on his side after all. His smile disappears.

"Could I have just 10 or 20 rupees?" he asks.

I turn my back on him again and push my way through the crowd. As I walk towards the Enquiry window, people guess my intent. They shout out the names of possible destinations. The young man, still at my hip, tries to guess my destination too.

I ignore them and head towards the window, my salvation. When I get there, however, the Enquiry window is deserted.

"Lunch!" someone from the crowd yells. They laugh hungrily, and press even closer. I begin to fear that someone might cut open my bag – I read about this – so I put it on the ground between the wall and myself. People continue to laugh and shout out destinations, hoping to guess correctly. Other members of the crowd push the young man forward and egg him on in Hindi.

"Give me money," he demands. People laugh and push him forward. "Give me money."

What little strength I had was tied up in the idea that the person at the Enquiry window would help me. Now, I'm alone, facing a hostile crowd and this man. I brace myself for a fight I can't win. I haven't felt this small and alone since I was eight years old, surrounded by older kids who were teasing me, hoping to see me cry.

I'm saved by the shout of "Igatpurri!" The fact that someone knows the name of my destination fills me with relief. I no longer feel so alone.

"Yes," I reply.

An Indian man wearing a white turban steps forward.

"Ten days meditation course," he asks.

"Yes!" I say, feeling stress drain from my body. Maybe he's a meditator too.

"The train is not until 3:00." His honesty cements my feeling of comfort with him.

"I know," I tell him, looking him in the eye and trying to communicate the fact that we are now on the same side.

"There is a bus," he says.

"What time?"

"Every hour. One at 12:00. One at 1:00."

"How long is it?"

"About 4 hours."

Even if I miss the 12:00 bus, I can still make the 1:00 and be at Igatpurri by 5:00.

"Can you take me there?"

Of course he can. "It's a short ride," he says. "Follow me."

The crowd grows silent as we speak and now that I'm officially with someone, they make room for us to pass. The laughter and the guessing have stopped, but the 18-year-old pest hasn't given up yet. He takes one last swipe at my bag and when he misses, he walks alongside us. When we get outside, he turns towards me again.

"Let me have just 10 rupees," he says.

I've had all I can take.

"Get the hell away from me!" I shout.

The young man opens his mouth to retort, but glances at my new companion and keeps quiet.

The three of us walk down the street where we meet another man, introduced as my guide's brother, and their taxicab. I'm relieved to see that the cab is clean and new.

When the brothers open the trunk, the young man grabs my bag once again, still hoping to assist me with it, but I pull it away. As I put my bag in the trunk, he runs to the side of the cab and opens the passenger side door. I consider slighting him and going to the other side, but then decide that the least he owes me for all the trouble he caused is to open a door for me.

I get in and he closes the door behind me. He looks at me hopefully and I give him a big, satisfied grin. I wave goodbye as we pull away, feeling a savage contentment that all his efforts were for naught. But I couldn't be more wrong. I have run from him directly into the arms of two con men. It seems I still have some bad Karma to work off.

9.

It goes without saying that I have no idea where the bus station is. I'm completely dependent upon these people to take me there and I trust that they will obey my wishes.

The two men inform me that they have taken many people to the meditation center. They know all about it and have great respect for people who go there.

"Where are you from?" they ask.

"America."

"How long have you been in India?"

"I just arrived yesterday."

"When will you go home?"

"I'm hoping to stay in India for about 5 to 6 months. I hear it's a beautiful country, and I'm hoping to get a chance to see a lot of it."

"What will you do while you are here?"

"I just want to try to get to know India. I plan to travel a lot, but I don't really have an itinerary."

The men nod and smile as I speak. I assume that this is idle talk, but it's not. In fact, these seemingly innocent questions are really attempts on their part to determine my level of vulnerability and economic worth. What they've learned is that I'm a con artist's dream: a foreigner who doesn't know India and has money to spend.

I notice that we've moved from a very busy and populated area to what begins to look like a slum. Soon there are no people in sight. Run down and deserted houses line the street. Abandoned cars lie on the side of the road. When we pull over and stop under a dark bridge, my heart begins to beat in my throat and I can hardly breathe.

"What are we doing?" I ask, trying not to sound nervous.

The two brothers turn to look at me.

"Would you like to take a private taxi?" the brother with the blue eyes and the turban asks in a tone of voice that is more statement than question.

I think about it for a moment. I hadn't expected this.

"How much would it cost?"

"Not more than 100 American dollars."

I gasp and almost laugh. That's 4,000 rupees, which I know is a small fortune here. I don't want to spend that much money on anything.

"No thank you. That's way too much money for me."

"Not more than $100," he repeats.

"No thank you," I say again. "Just take me to the bus station."

"How much would you pay?" he insists.

I've worked with salespeople before and I know something about haggling. If I name an amount, he'll mock me as if I've said something ludicrous, all the while using my response to gauge how high he can push the price. At any rate, this is a moot point as I don't want to pay for a private ride.

"It doesn't matter. I don't want a private car. Just take me to the bus station."

"How much would you pay," he repeats in his flat, serious voice.

"Look," I say, trying to be reasonable. "$100 is way too much for me. I don't have that kind of money. All I want to do is take the bus. Just take me to the station."

"Sir," he says in a voice which suggests I'm being unreasonable and cheap, "How much do you think is fair?"

It's obvious that they are not going to take me to the bus station. So, I take stock of my situation. We're in a deserted neighborhood, sitting under a dark bridge. No one knows where I am and there's no one around to shout to for help. My duffel bag, containing all my belongings, is locked in their trunk. I have all my money on my person, about $3,000 in traveler's checks and about 500 American dollars. I don't think they are going to hurt me – if they wanted to rob me there would be nothing to discuss – but I am at their mercy. It never occurred to me when I was in America, imagining this trip, that going without an itinerary or a guide would leave me so vulnerable to the manipulations of dishonest people.

I take a deep breath. I don't want to insult them or make them angry, but I need to find a way to get out of here, unhurt, and hopefully without getting too ripped off.

"I'd pay 1,000 rupees."

The men look at each other and share a laugh.

"Sir," the turbaned brother replies in an amused, patronizing voice, "that wouldn't pay for the gas. Be serious. How much?"

I smile, as they laugh, to show I mean no harm.

"I tried to tell you," I say, hoping he'll see how reasonable I've been, "I can't afford a private cab. 1,000 rupees is what I could afford. But it doesn't matter. I'd be happy to take the bus. Let's just go to the bus station, OK?"

"$75?"

"No thank you. I can't afford it. I just want to go to the bus station."

"$50?"

I pause to think about it. $50 is twice what I would want to pay, but I might pay $50 if it would get me to the meditation center and out of this situation. I decide I would if I had to, but I don't want to.

What I don't realize is that my hesitation indicates that I can afford to pay the $50. If it really was too much, there'd be nothing to think about.

"No thanks," I say, still hoping I can turn this into a reasonable conversation. "I really can't afford to pay for a private car."

"$50," he insists. "2,000 rupees."

Again I pause, and he senses victory is near. Just one more push…

"You can pay half now and half when you get there."

This convinces me. The idea that I can hold half the fare over their heads until we arrive at my destination appeals to me, even if paying 2,000 rupees doesn't.

"OK. I'll do it. Can we go now?"

They smile at me.

"One moment sir." He starts the car and we pull out from under the bridge. I feel relief wash over me. I'm still at their mercy, but at least we're out in the open again.

We drive to a more populated residential area. People are outside walking the streets and the houses look lived in. I feel much safer.

We pull over and the turbaned brother gets out and runs down the street.

"Where is he going?" I ask the remaining brother.

"One moment sir."

"What are we doing here?"

"One moment sir."

My illusion of being in charge vanishes. I have no choice but to wait this out and see what they have in store for me.

"Have you seen the Jain temple?"

"What?"

"The Jain temple. Have you seen it?"

"No."

"Oh, well, you really should. It's beautiful."

"Uh, okay."

"And, what about Elephanta Island?"

"No."

"Oh, sir, you have to see that. It is really amazing. You'll love it. I promise you."

"Maybe next time."

As he tries to make small talk, I have to restrain myself from lunging over the seat and strangling him. It's bad enough that he's ripping me off. Does he have to pretend to be my friend too?

After a 10-minute delay the brother returns and we drive off. Once again we enter an uninhabited area and I wonder if I'm going to get robbed now. Maybe he asked some friends to meet us at a deserted location.

Indeed, there is a man waiting for us. We pull over and the turbaned brother gets out and speaks with him. After a few minutes the man knocks on my window and motions for me to get out. I open the door and get out warily, prepared to defend myself.

"This man will drive you," the brother informs me.

"I thought you two were taking me?"

The brothers share an amused smile. Aren't tourists cute?

"No, sir. This man will drive you."

"Where is his car?"

"Right here," he says, pointing in the direction of an abandoned, beat up vehicle.

"Where?"

"Right here," he says again, pointing in the same direction.

Suddenly, I understand. And at the same time I don't. That car isn't going anywhere. It's just a rusted metal shell. Surely they're joking.

They're not joking. The men put my backpack in the trunk of the car and I walk around it. The car has no mirrors. Neither side nor rear view. The gauges are all cracked. There are no seat belts. I've never seen a dirtier or more rusted vehicle. Does it really work?

The lead brother opens the rear door and I reluctantly sit inside. The seat, while ripped and torn, has a small bit of padding left to sit on.

He closes the door behind me, and I notice that there are no door lock knobs. None of the doors have them. I wonder if I've just been imprisoned in the car. I pull the door handle and am relieved to discover that it does open. It simply doesn't lock.

I search the car, while the men continue to talk, and find a detached window handle lying in the front seat. I grab it, at first because I think I can use it as a weapon. I soon realize that we have to use this to open any of the windows in the car. Each door still has the knob that the handle fits into, but only this one handle remains. I insert the handle into my door and roll down the window, just to see if it works.

The turbaned brother comes over to my window.

"You pay me 1,600 rupees now," he demands.

"No," I say immediately. "We agreed on half now and half when I reach Igatpurri. 1,000 now."

"Sir," he says in a pained voice, "You pay 1,600 now. When you reach Igatpurri you pay the driver 400. If you like the service, then you pay 500 or 600. Okay?"

It's not okay. He's stealing my precious leverage. But it's only an illusion anyway.

"He knows where he's going?" I ask, defeated again.

The man nods and waits for the money with an outstretched hand.

I turn away from him, trying to hide the contents of my fanny pack from his view. I don't want him to see how much money I have on me. Very carefully, I pull out three 500-rupee bills and one 100-rupee bill. I count it twice silently and then hand it to him. The man takes the money and counts it. He then puts his hand back in the car and holds the money out for me to see.

"Sir..." he says suggestively.

I look at his hand and am horrified. He's holding two 500-rupee bills and two 100-rupee bills. It's meant to look as if I made a simple mistake and gave him a 100-rupee bill instead of a 500-rupee bill, but I wonder why he's even bothered with this charade. He's cheating me again and I can't stop him. How can I argue with what's in his hand?

My hand shakes when I take the money from him. I take out another 500-rupee bill and count the money out loud. This time, when I give him the money, he takes it without comment.

The driver gets in and starts the engine. I grip the window handle tightly in my hand, hoping desperately I can just get away from here. But before we go, the brother comes back to my window.

"Sir," he says. "Some money for our troubles."

"What?" I want to cry and strike him at the same time.

"A tip for our help."

"You must be kidding. I just gave you 1,600 rupees." Actually, I gave him 2,000 rupees, but who's counting?

"Sir," he persists. "For good luck on your journey. Just 100 rupees more."

Even though English isn't his primary language, he's managed to master the art of the subtle threat. I know what good luck on my journey means. One word in Hindi from him and the driver will take me to Timbuktu. I give him the extra 100.

"Thank you," he smiles and walks away.

I sit back and try to relax between the ripped out pieces of foam. The driver starts the engine, and we pull away. I'm relieved to see the two men disappear into the distance. I only hope the driver knows where he's going.

10.

If you have never seen the chaos that passes for normal road traffic in India you will never be able to understand the true horror of it all. First, the streets overflow with cars and busses which swerve recklessly between lanes at full speed. Second, there appear to be only a few traffic laws governing the conduct of moving vehicles: honk at anything that moves or potentially might move; drive in any lane you want to, including lanes where vehicles are traveling in the opposite direction (as long as you are honking, people will know you are there and will be able to avoid you); and, if you can't avoid a pothole, run through it at the highest possible speed. Then, there's the fact that the animals have escaped the zoo. Cows, dogs, donkeys, sheep, and monkeys roam the streets at will. These also need to be avoided – especially the cows, which are sacred.

This would be stressful in a working cab, but I feel much worse when I realize his gauges are broken. The fuel needle never moves from empty. The speedometer reads 10 kilometers per hour whether we are going 100 or standing still. I am convinced that nothing but the gas and the brakes work (thank God for the brakes!). I was actually safer while trapped under the bridge.

I do my best to meditate in the bumpy back seat and manage to calm myself a bit. Then, the moment I begin to relax I see the Indian version of a "buckle up" sign. It reads, "The view of a hospital ceiling is not very interesting, you really don't want to spend the next few months looking at it" and I realize that this insanity really is as dangerous as it seems. And part of the insanity is that the sign should have been written in Hindi instead of English! Who are they trying to warn? Me?

When I can no longer take the fear, I start making deals with God over how much tip I will give this man if he gets me to the center alive – I'll give him 100, no 200 rupees. God's response: it starts to rain.

The rain comes down in thick sheets so heavy and hard that I can't see more than three feet in front of the cab. In addition, our windshield wipers don't work, so the driver thrusts one hand out the window in order to try to clear the windshield with a dirty handkerchief. Despite the three feet of visibility, his speed doesn't diminish at all. He just keeps honking his horn, squinting out the window and wiping furiously with his left hand. If another car stops in front of us we are going to die.

I swear to God that if I get there alive I'll give him a 1,000-rupee bill.

At some point during this hell I look at my watch and realize that it is no longer working. I'm either in a twilight zone where time stops at 1:30 and people are suicidal maniacs, or I am having a very bad day.

Eventually the rain stops and I see signs pointing the way to Igatpurri. He does know where he's going after all! We are going to make it! I try to tell him he doesn't have to hurry, but he doesn't understand. Even though he won't slow down and the possibility of a fatal accident is still high, I'm deliriously happy.

After 3½ hours we arrive, all in one piece. I give him 1,000 rupees – 2½ times what he was expecting to receive. He practically jumps out of his shoes with joy. My knees are so weak I can hardly walk up the path to the main building. I've never been more relieved to be anywhere.

As I calm down, I realize that the driver was being neither especially reckless nor especially courageous. What we'd been through had been quite normal for him. In fact, he was going to return home and do it all over again. What had happened wasn't remarkable at all. It was just India.

Igatpurri

People generally react with horror when I tell them about the meditation retreats I have done. At first, I felt intimidated too. The beginning level course, in this tradition, is a 10-day silent retreat. The length of time, in itself, is daunting, but it's the silence that seems to unnerve people the most. "I could never stay silent for ten days," is a common refrain. I know the feeling. We are so ubiquitously surrounded by distractions that most of us have never had the experience of truly sitting in silence, looking deep inside and examining what happens beneath our surface awareness. Freud called it the unconscious, but our meditation instructor rejects this very concept. "The mind is conscious all the time," he says, "you just don't know how to be aware of its' depth." The idea that we could be aware of everything that goes on in our minds, that we could understand why we do seemingly irrational and incomprehensible things, can be intimidating as well, but without exploring the depths of our minds, how can we ever truly know who we are?

I gravitated toward meditation because Buddhism claims that meditation is a way out of a life of suffering, and I knew I was suffering. I carried emotional pain from my childhood. It colored how I saw my world, made me feel anxious and vulnerable, and I didn't know how to be free of its influence. I had also seen how my father's own anguish had made him, and the rest of my family, miserable. My meditation teacher says, rightly, that people never keep their pain to themselves, but get busy with the process of spreading their misery. When my father came home from work, exhausted and bitter, he'd lash out at us like an exploding volcano, and we never knew who would get burned. His unhappiness burdened us all, and I didn't want to mimic his behavior. But it was my grandmother's example that truly motivated me to do something about my emotional wounds.

A few years after my grandfather died, my grandmother moved into an assisted living home, in Florida, with her two remaining sisters. They were all widowers, whose children had lives and families of their own. They lived on the same hall, and for a while it was blissful. When my family would visit, the three sisters would talk excitedly like schoolgirls, all speaking at the same time, none of them listening to each other, yet all of them happy just to be alive and to be together.

Over time this began to change.

"Mom always liked you better."

"You always got the nice dresses."

"You used to steal my boyfriends."

Hurts and grudges over seventy years old resurfaced, and the pain of these memories was somehow unabated despite the long intervening years. They began to fight and argue over these ancient events, and before long the sisters stopped speaking to each other. They grew apart, as their childhood pain forced them to live alone, isolated and bitter, despite the fact they lived on the same hallway.

The idea that childhood pain could fester and be undiminished despite decades of time terrified me. I already carried as much pain as I could manage. I knew I would be destined to be as bitter and angry as my father if it continued to build. I had to find a way out, and meditation, in theory, offered a way to eliminate suffering.

I know that most people, if interested in something new, would go slowly. Maybe take an hour course, or maybe a package of several hours over a couple of weeks time. Who would jump into a 10-day silent retreat?

I would. In fact, I wouldn't do it any other way. When it comes to the things that are most important in life, I don't understand compromise. If I'm going to learn a spiritual practice, I want to learn something that people dedicate their lives to. I want a technique that can scrub my soul clean, and help me bear whatever I find there. The fact that this group offered nothing less than a 10-day introductory retreat told me how seriously they felt about their practice. The fact that they offered it for free, told me how priceless they believed it to be. I attended two courses in Massachusetts in the year before I journeyed to India. I experienced the miracle of what they offer, and I desperately hope I'll be able to experience it again.

2.

The enormous Indian meditation center, located in the remote rural village of Igatpurri, occupies acres of grassy, flat land. The train, which I was erroneously told did not run from Victoria Station, passes noisily by every few hours, but it's the only reminder of the world I left behind.

Three hundred Indian men and women participate in the 10-day course I've enrolled in, while hundreds of people from concurrent courses (the center offers 10-day, 20-day, 30-day, 45-day, and 60-day retreats), pass by during mealtimes, on their way to and from the gigantic cafeteria. Three large meditation halls provide communal meditation space, and a giant pagoda – a large tapering golden cone – which I am told, holds several hundred individual meditation cells, dominates the pale blue skyline. During break times, hordes of anonymous students walk quietly along the numerous dirt walking paths, which wind over gently sloping green hills and in between sparse, skinny trees. The center has full time chefs, several dormitories, and even an Indian style laundromat where you can pay a few rupees to have Indian women wash your clothes. This is not some off-the-beaten-track refuge for oddball Westerners who want to learn meditation, but a thriving meditation metropolis.

My group of 300 spends most of its time in one of the meditation halls: a large, open, square building with hundreds of blue meditation mats lining the floor. I sit in the third row from the front, and I have the only meditation bench at the center. I thought everyone in India would have one of these, but only I do. This means I literally sit head and shoulders above everyone else – a fact I try to ignore, as I really don't want to stand out.

Our instructions for the first three days are to be aware of our breath as it flows in and out of our nostrils. The head teacher explains that we should be conscious of whether it is soft or hard, long or short. Nothing else. Simply sharpen our awareness of this natural process.

It sounds simple, but it is very difficult. Based on my previous experiences, I know I have to be calm and relaxed to feel my breath, but my mind refuses to cooperate. When I close my eyes, I see the mocking face of the young man who chased me across the highway and the condescending blue eyes of the turbaned brother who forced me to pay for a private ride. I try to focus on my breathing, but my mind returns again and again to the fear and humiliation of feeling helpless, manipulated, and abused. I angrily wrest my mind from these visions, only to find myself embroiled in fantasies of revenge. Now, instead of being intimidated, I grapple with the young man, fight him while surrounded by excited Indian men, cheering for blood. Or, I confidently demand that the two brothers take me to the bus station as promised, intimating that I'm amused by their pathetic attempts to cow me. Remembering that I'm sitting in a cool, dark meditation hall, free from harassment and danger, is a difficult and frustrating challenge.

Still, I remind myself that this is natural and healthy. The only way to diminish the pain I experienced while being pushed around is to allow myself to feel it. By sitting with my pain, without reacting to it or repressing it, I slowly allow that energy to dissipate. And, in fact, over the three days we practice the breathing meditation my pain lessens, my mind stops worrying about what happened and slowly settles into my current, safe, reality. I feel less anxious, and the memories become less painful. If nothing else, it feels good to sit in the silence and let go of the tension of my Indian adventure.

I'm excited when, on the fourth day, the teacher announces that we are going to move into Vipassana meditation. This is ultimately why we all have come here, and I feel ready.

Vipassana is a word in an ancient Indian language, called Pali, which the head teacher translates to mean "true insight." Through Vipassana, we strive to delve beneath our surface thoughts and discover what lies in our depths so we can truly begin to understand who we are. We used the breath as a bridge to get from our regular, conscious awareness of ourselves, to that which is normally unconscious. The breath is a perfect vehicle for this because it exists in both worlds; although we can control our breath, if we ignore it, it continues unconsciously. By learning to follow uncontrolled breath, we teach our mind to travel from what we consciously can control, to those aspects of our reality that are not controlled. As our awareness becomes more and more subtle, we notice not only how hard or fast we are breathing, but also find that subtle sensations cover our whole body.

Generally speaking, we only notice very intense sensations. After sitting in a room for 30 minutes, we notice that it's gotten cold and we put on a sweater. What we don't consciously realize is that the room had been getting colder the whole time. The chill began as a subtle physical sensation and a part of our mind monitored it until it grew sufficiently intense for us to feel the need to do something about it. It's the same thing for an itching sensation on our nose, or a cramp in our calf. Throughout, an "unconscious" part of our mind monitors the sensation from the moment it began, noticed how it increased in intensity, and finally decided when it was time to act.

Through the bridge of our breath, we spent the first three days of the retreat attempting to access the part of the mind which constantly feels subtle body sensations, and once we developed this level of awareness, we worked to increase it, until we could feel sensations, gross and subtle, over the entire surface of the body. They always existed, but at a level of consciousness that we were heretofore unaware of.

The secret power of this technique is that these physical sensations are inextricably tied to our inner reality. The mind and body are not separate, as we generally believe, but are two inseparable, intertwined aspects of our being – mind does not exist independent of body. Whenever I get angry, for example, my body responds. I may clench my fists. I may grind my teeth. I may feel a sensation of heat. But body and mind react together. In the same manner, we all know that the mind stores memories of events and emotions. What we may not realize is that we also store the physical sensations that accompanied these memories and emotions. If I remember getting angry, I will likely clench my fists, grind my teeth, and feel heat, just as I did when the actual event happened. There is no separation between mind and body.

So, when I am able to be aware of the body's subtle sensations, which had been unconscious, I can simultaneously be aware of what happens mentally and emotionally beneath the surface of my normal, day-to-day experience of life. What was hidden in the unconscious reveals itself to conscious awareness. An intense sensation will rise to the surface of my mind/body, and with it will be whatever emotion or thought or feeling it connects to – a painful memory that had been long forgotten may resurface, or something more subtle, perhaps a feeling of mild frustration that I had this morning when I dropped a piece of bread on the floor. As I am aware of new sensations, the unprocessed emotional material that accompanies the physical sensation may rise to the level of my conscious attention. Then I can sit with it, the same way I sat with my memories of the taxi drivers, and over time, the intensity of feelings and pain will slowly pass away, until I can remember the painful or traumatic event without having to re-experience the pain that accompanied it.

I have experienced this before, and am eager to begin again. Not only do I want to further expunge the pain from the last few days, but I hope I can delve into deeper pain and heal wounds that might be blocking me from discovering who I really am and what I truly want. Unlocking those mysteries may finally lead me to happiness, or at least to a job that I can enjoy. I have to believe that I am just a moment away from finding the answer. When I no longer believe this, I'll have no choice but to return home, discard my dreams, and get a "real" job. Just like my father. The very idea feels like a slow, enervating, death. Coming all this way, taking this leap of faith, has to pay off. Doesn't it?

3.

Nothing's happening. Nothing at all. And I think I'm going to lose my mind.

In normal life, an endless stream of changing experiences breaks up the monotony of existence. I have things to do, places to go, people to see. These innumerable enticing distractions help the day pass quickly and painlessly, and I wonder where all the time went.

But here, nothing changes. Our meditation schedule lasts from 4:30 in the morning to 9:00 at night, which means, taking into account meal and break times, we sit and meditate for 12 hours per day. And, every day is the same. Every hour, the same. Every moment – virtually the same. At 4:30 AM my job is exactly the same as it is at 9:00 PM. I focus my attention on awareness of each breath, each sensation, as it arises, as it passes away, sometimes itching, sometimes tingling, sometimes heat, sometimes pain – just notice and be as aware and focused as I can be. There are no television shows, no daily tasks, no conversations to break up this endless horizon of plodding time. When I can feel and focus on sensations, when I can embrace reality's moment-to-moment, breath-by-breath truth, morning turns into night in a gradual, peaceful, laconic seeming haze.

When my mind can't feel sensations, however, time doesn't seem to pass at all. In fact, when I can't feel sensations all I can do is think about time – how much has passed, how many days before the course ends, how many hours before lunch, when can I go to sleep.

I sit in the hall, after breakfast on day five of the course, and try to be aware of what's happening on my face, a location where sensations generally explode into my consciousness, but it's completely blank. So are my arms, my neck, and my torso. Same with my back and my legs. Without sensations to concentrate on, my mind drifts away. I pull it back and force it to focus on a body part, and it wanders away again. I try again. And again. With the same aggravating results. Finally, after what seems like hours, I allow myself to look at my watch – only to discover that barely twenty minutes have passed. I still have eight hours to go before I can go to sleep. And after that I get to wake up at the crack of dawn and try again.

There's nothing to distract me from the fact that I sit in a silent hall, as hour passes hour, surrounded by Buddha-like meditators, doing absolutely nothing. And hating every single, solitary, drawn out moment.

The center's master teacher, for his part, reminds us that this is normal.

"The mind is bound to wander away," he says. When it does, he advises us to "smilingly" return our focus to the meditation. It's even possible to feel no sensation at all, he says, a benevolent smile on his face. "Just observe," he advises, and "keep trying. Continuous effort is the secret of success"

I want to shake his calm, compassionate demeanor from his fat, smiling face. I'm not a beginner! I know how to do this. My mind shouldn't wander away. I should be able to feel sensations all over my body. That advice has nothing to do with me!

I force myself to sit in the hall for two more hours, desperately searching my body for the smallest indication that I *can* feel something somewhere. But somehow, even though my legs are cramped and tired and sore, when I focus my mind there I can't even feel the pain.

I decide to go to the large golden pagoda, where I have a private meditation cell, hoping a change of locations will help. I enter the cramped 4x6x6 room, arrange cushions in the most comfortable position I can, sit calmly with my back straight, plaster a saint-like passivity on my face (if I look like the Buddha, maybe I can meditate like him), and calmly focus my mind. But I sit for two more hours and still can't feel a thing. Finally, I'm left, exhausted, to count the cracks in the wall (ten minutes pass), give myself mental lectures on how useless I am (a good waste of fifteen minutes), or fall asleep (ultimately, the only way I can make it to bedtime).

Two days later, my back hurts, my legs ache, and I feel like crying. No wonder this is free!

In my daydreams, my friends imagine I'm having a wonderful time. They gather at a fancy restaurant, open a bottle of wine, and discuss my latest escape from real life. "Don't you just envy Jason?" they say as they sip their Chianti. "He must be having so much fun. Right now, he's supposed to be at the meditation center. Wouldn't it be nice to be able to take time off and just relax?"

I want to scream at them. I'm busting my ass trying to achieve enlightenment. You're at home taking it easy! Which one of us is relaxing?

And I wonder angrily; why aren't I relaxing? I came here to unwind. What difference does it make if my mind wanders away or if it's not sharp enough to feel the body's sensations? Why do I struggle so?

I hate to give up. I have learned to use a stubborn refusal to quit to overcome my habitual lack of self-confidence. I believe that if I know I won't give up, I'll have no choice but to give the task at hand all the effort I can muster. But I realize, in this case, that it's foolish to continue to make myself miserable just so I can say I persevered. If I can't meditate, maybe that's not the most important thing. What I really need is to relax and get some peace and quiet. Enough, at least, so I can head back out into India and continue my trip. That is the minimum I need from this retreat. It's not what I hoped for, but it will be better than going home after two weeks because I couldn't deal with the stress of being in India.

It's difficult at first, but I sit in the meditation hall in the morning of day six and force myself to stop panicking when I discover that I can't feel sensations. I remind myself to just accept my meditation however it is. An hour later, when I tire of sitting in the meditation hall, I allow myself to go outside and listen to the birdsong, watch a nearby hill where the local shepherd walks his flock of sheep, or idly observe leaves fluttering in the breeze. By the time our lunch break ends, I can feel myself starting to relax. I am no longer fixated on the need to have success in meditation. And something very strange happens. When I go back into the meditation hall, I can feel tingling in my face and legs. I try to restrain my excitement, sit calmly and scan my body. Soon, sensations arise on my hands and arms, and by the end of the hour, I can feel subtle vibrations on my torso. Suddenly, I can sit in the hall, pass my attention through my body and feel sensations everywhere. I can meditate again. The torture is over.

I had thought that pushing myself to try harder would enable me to achieve the success I desired, but it was only after I stopped pushing myself that I was able to actually meditate. At first it seems counterintuitive, but over the next few days, I realize how destructive my need to strive for perfection, in everything, has been for me. I had told myself that it motivated me to work hard and that perfection was a healthy and worthwhile goal, but I understand now that this was a ruse. It was, in fact, a trap set up by my own subconscious insecurity.

There is a deep part of my psyche that does not like who I am. Years of feeling disapproved of, believing that my parents never took my opinion or feelings into account, being the subject of random attacks by my father, being picked on by schoolmates and teachers at school, and never being protected, led to the development of an internal belief that something is wrong with me. I believe I am bound to be deserted by my friends, bound to be disliked by those who meet or know me. This is not all that I believe, of course. There is also a part of my psyche which values who I am, but these two beliefs are in conflict, and it is often the negative valance that wins. I had convinced myself that striving for perfection was a way to fight against my negative self-image, but I now understand that it was internal sabotage intended to prove that my negative self-image is correct.

I imagine that there is a healthy kind of perfection, where a person works to make the perfect expression of his craft. Such a person would feel uplifted when he accomplished this goal, but he would understand that perfection is achieved only rarely, even by the most skilled of craftsmen.

For the most part, people are imperfect, and to expect perfection from each and every action is to set oneself up for failure.

Which is exactly what I have been doing. My need to be perfect was not restricted to those actions I was especially skilled at, but extended to every aspect of my life. When I started a new job, for example, I demanded that I do every task perfectly after it had been explained to me once. I would revile myself for any misspoken word, no matter how slight, or any deed, no matter how insignificant, which failed to live up to my imagined standard of perfection.

If I did manage to do something perfectly, I saw this accomplishment as merely adequate, and promptly moved onto something else without giving myself any credit for my success. I felt no better about myself, experienced no satisfaction, even after I achieved perfection. This was a sure sign that my need for perfection was unhealthy. Meditation helped me realize that needing to be perfect actually made perfection more difficult to achieve because that very pressure and strain weighs my mind down and restricts its ability to function optimally. By demanding that I meditate deeper than ever before, I put pressure on myself, and the moment I struggled, I became afraid that I was too feebleminded to achieve my intended goal. This fear, this pressure, hindered my mind's ability to operate at full capacity, and thus impeded my ability to achieve my goal. Giving up the goal of perfection, being focused, yet relaxed, allowed me to optimize my performance.

The head teacher often tells us that we are learning an "Art of Living," and I understand now that he is speaking the plain truth.

4.

The code of silence lifts the day before the end of the course. The idea is to provide a "shock absorber" so that meditators won't be released into the world before they remember how to socialize with others. It's an exciting time where we finally get to meet the people who sat next to us and discover who else is so strange as to want to endure a 10-day silent meditation retreat.

I walk towards the cafeteria, eager to enjoy our first talking lunch, when a group of Indian men approaches me.

"Where are you from?" one man shouts excitedly.

"America," I reply.

"What are you doing in India?" another man asks.

"I'm not sure. I've never been here before. I want to travel. Maybe I'll try some yoga. I don't really know."

The man turns his head and translates my answer into Hindi. After a pause, someone shouts out another question in Hindi, and he translates.

"How long will you be staying here?"

"For about five months."

"Where will you be going?"

"I'm not sure."

"Where did you get that bench?"

"I brought it here from America. I thought many people here would have them?"

"Oh, no. That would be very expensive. Can I see it?"

"Sure." I hand it to the translator, and he passes it around. People murmur excitedly. It's lifted, admired, measured. I worry that it's more popular than I am. (Who knew I could have bench envy?).

Over the next few hours, I wander the center and speak to many of my co-meditators. I hope to receive some sort of guidance. I need to figure out what I should do next.

Two of the men I meet stand out from the rest. The first is a young man in his early thirties named Niranjan. I don't feel a particular connection with him, but whenever I'm in a group of people, I notice that he's there, watching me. I haven't forgotten my recent ordeals in Mumbai, and I'm wary. What does this guy want?

It isn't long before Niranjan asks about my plans.

"I don't really have any plans," I admit reluctantly.

"You might want to visit Nasik," he replies, almost managing to make it sound casual. "It's close to the meditation center, and there are famous Hindu temples and Buddhist caves there. Many tourists go there. It's worth the trip."

Later, he overhears me asking people about yoga teachers.

"It just so happens," he tells me, "that I have a close friend who is an expert yoga instructor. If you come to Nasik I'll introduce you."

Eventually, he reveals his agenda.

"Would you like to come with me to Nasik? I have a place where you can stay. I can even give you a key. It would be like your own place. I'll show you around Nasik and you can have dinner at my house and meet my family."

Now I really begin to worry. Am I supposed to believe that this man followed me around the center so that he can be generous to me? It must be a set up, and I don't want to be forced to pay for another "private ride." I decide to avoid him whenever I can.

In fact, it's while I take a seldom-used path, hoping to escape Niranjan's prying eyes, that I meet the old man.

He's a thin Indian gentleman, wearing brown dress slacks and a white button down dress shirt. He stands up gingerly when he sees me. "Will you sit with me a moment?" he asks, sunlight glinting off his thick spectacles. "I've been looking for you. My name is Dr. Rama Mad Mahi. Of course, I saw you sitting on that bench. I don't know why, but I felt a closeness to you. Like we've been friends for a long time. I want to give you an open invitation to come and stay with my wife and myself in Nasik."

"Thank you," I say quickly. My impulse is to humor the nice old man, let him think I'd like to do that sometime and then never take him up on his offer. Because I neither trust people, nor have confidence in myself, I generally avoid strangers – even well meaning ones. But, as I watch him write down his phone number and address in patient, clear handwriting, I take stock of my situation. I came to India because I want to step out of my old anxiety-laden skin. I know I would like to be the kind of person who isn't defensive and afraid, the kind of person who would allow a well meaning stranger to be kind to him. My life is full of regrets, replete with situations when I demurred and avoided potentially positive experiences. Now, a man offers to show me his life, give me an idea what it's like to live in India. If I can't allow this old man to be nice to me, when will I ever allow anyone to do so?

"Well…" I begin, trying to throw caution aside. "I don't know if this will work, but I have time when the course ends."

He pauses mid writing, stunned, but then smiles.

"Yes," he says. "I have room in my car, so you can leave the center with me. I have the next few days off from work. Yes!" He shakes my hand vigorously. "This will work out perfectly. Let me go call my wife!"

He hurries away, and my habitual nervousness returns. I don't know anything about this man. I don't know anything about Nasik. I have no idea what I have just gotten myself into. Then again, I reassure myself, at least I've found a good excuse to turn down Niranjan's offers.

Only it doesn't work out that way. Niranjan is very disappointed when I tell him I've made plans to visit Nasik with someone else. But then something strange happens. Niranjan tracks down the old man. They talk. They change the plan. The older man will give us both a ride into town. I'll stay at Niranjan's apartment. He'll show me around Nasik and together we'll have dinner with the old man and his wife. On the second night I'll have dinner with Niranjan's family. Everything has been worked out – a guided tour of Nasik, a place to stay, dinner – it's an ideal scenario: everything I could want but would never ask for. Only, I don't trust Niranjan…

Nasik

"I've worked for the air force for over twenty years," Dr. Mahi says, as we drive along the highway. "I'm a senior engineer, and I have a very good job. I get paid a good salary, and my colleagues respect me, but I'm going to retire soon. I'm getting old, and I think it's time to let younger people take over. Besides, it will be nice to spend more time with my wife and my children and grandchildren."

I sit in the front seat, and Dr. Mahi glances at me as he speaks. Niranjan is in the back, next to Tarun, a very large, young, Indian man that, just before we left the meditation center, Niranjan invited to come with us. Dr. Mahi was as surprised as I was, but for reasons that must have to do with Indian courtesy, he shook Tarun's hand and said nothing.

"That sounds wonderful," I say. "It must feel nice to be able to relax and retire."

"Well, it was nice to be needed. I really liked knowing that my time was spent doing something important. But I was a very short-tempered man. I was full of stress, and I was abusive to my secretary and also sometimes to my wife. I even had cross relations with my superiors. I was always arguing with people. A few years ago my wife suggested to me that I try taking a meditation course. She said that it might help me relax. I didn't want to go at first, but I got into a very serious disagreement with the head of the department and I found myself shouting and yelling at him during an important meeting. After that, I realized I needed to do something. I tried the course, feeling very unsure about the whole thing.

"As I'm sure you all know, it's an amazing experience. I'm a totally changed person. Everyone noticed. My secretary is happier. I get along with my bosses now. Even my wife says I am nicer to be around. Before I took the course I think I would have never retired, but now I think it would be nice to be doing other things. I want to enjoy my family. And now I get to make new friends too. I want to know what all your experiences have been. I know Jason took the course before, because you sat in the front. Was it like this for you?"

"Sort of," I say hesitantly. I remember how, after I completed my first course, I felt compelled to push everyone I knew to take one too. Not only did I benefit from the course, but I thought if my friends and family went, and if they gained as I did, then they would truly appreciate me. Unfortunately, no one followed my lead, and I think my insistence actually made people uncomfortable, defensive and therefore more reluctant to try. I worry that Dr. Mahi might alienate Niranjan and Tarun by pressuring them to be as enthusiastic as he is, and I don't want to make that mistake again.

"But not quite in the same way as for you," I continue. "I never expressed my anger. I don't think other people could tell how this changed me. But I do feel calmer inside. I feel happier than I did before."

"Yes." Dr. Mahi says, nodding his head enthusiastically. "It's the same for me. What about you guys? Was this your first course?"

"It was my first course," Tarun says. "I heard about it in South Africa, and decided that I'd try it while I was here.

"I'm South African by birth," Tarun continues in a loud, commanding voice. "But my parents came from India. They wanted to be able to offer me a better life, and they succeeded. Today I work as a model." He flexes his muscles and holds his chin high, posing for us. "Now, it's not as glamorous as it sounds. The hours are long and the conditions are sometimes very unpleasant. I bet none of you have ever spent eight hours at the beach posing in a bathing suit in the hot sun! It can be very difficult. But it does have its plusses, as you can probably imagine," he pauses suggestively, and I turn away to roll my eyes. I think he's playing to our fantasies in the hopes that we'll admire him. Even so, I can't help but imagine the dalliances with bathing suit clad beauties that he suggests happens in his industry. I don't really believe him, yet I envy him for the mere possibility that it's true.

"Anyway," he clears his throat, "I've decided to take some time off. Despite my success, I've begun to feel as if something is missing in my life. I've come to find my roots and reconnect to my Indian past. My dream is to work as a model here, as well as in South Africa. Maybe I can help raise people's consciousness in both parts of the world. We'll have to see how things work out. But, I'm proud to be Indian. I'm proud to finally be here. It's a dream come true."

"What did you think about the meditation?" Dr. Mahi persists.

"Well, I don't know," Tarun tries to meet my eyes, then looks at Niranjan for support. "It was all right, I guess. I'm looking forward to getting to know Hinduism better. That's what I'm really excited about."

"What about you, Niranjan?" Dr. Mahi says curtly, dismissing Tarun and glancing at Niranjan in the mirror. "Was this your first course?"

"Yes, it was. I liked it. It was very hard. I think I'll try to keep up a practice."

"Good. Very good," Dr. Mahi says approvingly. "And what do you do?"

"Um…well, I work in a factory. It's not very interesting." Niranjan blushes slightly. "Really. Um, I got married a month ago," he adds, "so I also have to get home to my wife."

"Very good." Dr. Mahi replies.

"Congratulations!" Tarun shouts, shaking his hand.

"Yeah. Congratulations." I search Niranjan's eyes, wondering what this means. He shifts uneasily in his seat and I can see that he doesn't want to talk about this. I'm suspicious. What kind of person leaves his new wife to go off by himself for 10 days? It seems like more evidence that I should be wary of him.

"What about you, Jason?" Dr. Mahi asks. "What brings you to India? Did you come to take the course?"

I instantly feel exposed and nervous. I can sense Dr. Mahi's unspoken desire – I'm supposed to be an advocate for the meditation, as he is, and confirm that meditation changed my life. This is true, but if I echo his statements I'll feel as if I'm putting myself on a pedestal, as if I were a meditation expert, and I'm not comfortable in this role. After all, I only just learned how to do it. In addition, I'm not sure what I should say about myself. As the only person in the car without a career, I feel like a child among men. Like Tarun, I want to impress my companions, but I don't want to lie or exaggerate to do so. I decide to present myself as a worldly traveler, hoping that this will seem respectable.

"Well, I like to travel," I say, raising my voice, trying to act as confidently as Tarun. "I've been to Europe and Central America, and I love to experience different cultures and meet new people. I came to India because I hear it's a very beautiful, very spiritual place. I don't know exactly what I'm going to do here, but I'm excited to try to see what India has to offer."

In the silence that follows, I search my companions' faces, looking to see how they received my story. They seem disinterested, but not judgmental. This is both a relief and a let down, which is the catch 22 situation I often find myself in. I avoid telling people the truth about what I think and feel and want, because I'm afraid they will judge me, yet when my generic, evasive story doesn't win me approval or interest, I'm disappointed. I know, on some level, that I have set this scenario up, that people unconsciously understand my evasiveness as a plea to be left alone, but my self esteem is so low that I worry that if I really tell my companions who I am they will regret taking me with them. I'm more comfortable listening and supporting others than I am being in the spotlight or risking exposing my own feelings. It's easy to settle into this role, and I spend the rest of the car ride encouraging others to talk, while secretly wishing I felt comfortable enough to share my own feelings honestly.

2.

Several hours later, we arrive in Nasik. With its crowded streets, run down buildings, and meandering cows, this town reminds me of a smaller, poorer version of Bombay.

"Can you bring them to my house at 6:30 tonight?" Dr. Mahi asks Niranjan when he drops us off.

"Sure," he replies. "6:30. We'll be there."

Niranjan leads Tarun and me to a squat, gray building. It looks like a giant concrete shoebox with a large, dented, silver metal door on one side. He unlocks the door and gestures for us to enter. Three grey metal cots, one lamp, two desks, and a buzzing, swarming multitude of little black insects haphazardly surround a short, young Indian man, who apparently lives here. Tarun and I are almost as surprised to see him as he is to see us.

Niranjan quickly launches into Hindi and explains the situation. When he finishes, the young man shakes our hands vigorously.

"This is Amish," Niranjan says. "He's very excited to have you both stay with him. I'm afraid I have to go and see my wife now," he says apologetically. "I'll come back later to take you to Dr. Mahi's."

"Okay," I say. "Thanks for giving us the place to stay."

"Thanks a lot. This means a lot to me," Tarun gives Niranjan a big hug.

"No problem," Niranjan replies, patting Tarun on the back. "Make yourselves at home. My cousin is really very happy to have you here too, so don't worry. I'll see you at 6:00. That should give us enough time to get to Dr. Mahi's."

He leaves, and we turn to Niranjan's cousin.

"Do you speak any English?" Tarun asks.

He blushes and looks at the ground. We look at each other and shrug our shoulders.

"I think I saw an outhouse outside," I tell Tarun. "I'm going to use it."

"Do you need some toilet paper?" he asks.

"Do you have some?" I ask, flushed with embarrassment and relief. "That would be awesome!"

During the meditation course I learned that Indians traditionally don't use toilet paper. Instead, they use water and their left hand to clean themselves. This explains why greetings are always with the right hand, and why they only use the right hand when they eat.

I discovered this the hard way. I was warned by a friend back at home that I should bring toilet paper to India. She insisted that there wouldn't be any, but I didn't believe her…until, that is, I entered the bathroom at the meditation center and realized that there really wasn't any. (I had my hands, of course, but didn't want to use them for that purpose). Fortunately, there was a little store where I was able to purchase enough to last the course. Tarun's offer greatly eases my mind, as I really have to go to the bathroom, but don't want to do it the "Indian" way.

The outhouse is a small closet sized room, where I quickly discover that toilet paper isn't the only thing missing in Indian bathrooms. The toilets are also missing. The meditation center had an American (or Western, as it's called) toilet, but here, as I'll learn is common in India, the bathroom consists of a keyhole shaped hole in the ground, with two foot shaped markers, indicating where you should place your feet while you squat over the hole. I realize that if I'm going to be here, I'll have to get used to this kind of thing. I hold my breath and look down the hole, hoping to see nothing. Instead I can see that something is gently bobbing in the depths.

I know, from my experience in the meditation center, to look for a little faucet near the floor and an accompanying bucket. I fill the bucket with water, squat over the hole, close my eyes and try to concentrate on anything other than the buzzing of the flies and the smell emanating from the hole. When I'm finished, I use the toilet paper, throw it in the hole, wash my hands with the water from the bucket, and hightail it out of there.

At 6:30 Dr. Mahi opens the door to his apartment, and the three of us step into a lavish living room. Beautiful wooden cupboards and tall china cabinets line the walls, a lush light brown carpet covers the floor, and a plush orange couch, surrounded by two dark brown leather reclining chairs, occupies the center of the room. Everything sparkles as if it has just been cleaned or polished.

"Please sit down," Dr. Mahi says, his left arm sweeping towards the couch. "My wife will bring some sweets in a moment."

Tarun, Niranjan, and I sink into the couch, Dr. Mahi settles into one of the leather chairs, and Dr. Mahi's wife enters with a tray of fruit and tea.

"So," Dr. Mahi begins, kicking his feet up, "tell me Jason. What really brings you to India?"

"I don't know, exactly," I'm instantly on guard, surprised and nervous to be put on the spot. Why is he asking *me*?

"Surely you didn't come all the way to India without knowing. You must have some purpose."

"Well, it's kinda hard to say. I mean, I wanted to visit India. I know it's supposed to be a very spiritual place. I was hoping to meet people, like you and Niranjan, you know, get to know what it's really like here…" I look to Tarun for help.

"That's why I'm here as well." Tarun squares his shoulders, holds his head high, and raises his voice as he speaks. He's clearly rehearsed how he wants to act when he's in the spotlight. "India is the land of my ancestors. Though I fit in well in South Africa, I always felt something was missing. I always knew I had to come to India and learn about my heritage. I'm planning on going to Chennai, where I still have some family. I can't tell you how exciting it is for me to be here, and I am so grateful to you for having me over for dinner. It's my first real Indian meal in India!"

Dr. Mahi politely asks about Tarun's family in Chennai. I listen with everyone else, but behind my engaged façade I feel embarrassed because I know I'm hiding behind Tarun. I'd like to share my thoughts and feelings too, but I'm worried about being judged. Would Dr. Mahi respect me if he knew I had no career and was trying to find myself, or would he think, as my father does, that it is the action of a naïve, spoiled child?

We listen to Tarun's story, until Dr. Mahi's wife indicates that dinner is ready.

"We have silverware, if you like." Dr. Mahi's wife smiles at me kindly, her slim hands hovering near a cupboard.

"No thanks," I reply. "I had a chance to practice eating with chapattis during the meditation course. I think I can do it."

"I don't need silverware either," Tarun assures her.

"Okay." she says. "But, it's no problem if you change your mind."

The five of us sit around a long wooden table, while Dr. Mahi's wife spoons steaming vegetables onto multicolored china. Everything shines brightly, and simply oozes expensive taste.

"Please eat," she says once everyone has a plate of food.

I pick up a chapatti, a round piece of bread Indians use in lieu of silverware, and glance out of the corner of my eye to see if I'm being observed. Mrs. Mahi, elegantly dressed in a white and gold sari, seems poised on the edge of her seat, prepared to jump up and hand me silverware. Dr. Mahi, his thick spectacles glistening in the table light, also watches me intently. Even Niranjan, a kind smile on his face, watches my attempt to eat. Only Tarun, focused on his own food, seems to be oblivious to my performance.

During the meditation course I watched Indian meditators use chapattis to scoop up pieces of vegetables or mouthfuls of rice, making a sort of small chapatti sandwich. Because they only use their right hand, they have to break apart the chapatti single handed, which is tricky at first. But I had ten days of practice, and by the end I felt I could manage reasonably well. I break apart the bread, hold it between my thumb and middle finger, and squeeze it onto a mixture of potatoes and peas. I'm afraid I'll spill peas onto my nice khaki pants, or blue button down shirt, but somehow the food makes it to my mouth.

I look up, and Mrs. Mahi smiles at me. "Very good," Dr. Mahi, says nodding his approval. Niranjan also nods politely, and digs into his own food.

Now that I have avoided making a fool out of myself, we all dive into our dinner. At first, I marvel at the explosion of taste. "This is amazing!" I tell Mrs. Mahi, and she beams happily at me. After a few bites, however, my senses become overwhelmed. The eggplant is too spicy. The potatoes are too greasy. I can feel my stomach getting a little queasy. I'm a small and skinny man. I often inadvertently insult my hosts because I'm a light eater. I know that Mrs. Mahi will think I don't like the meal if I don't at least finish what she has given me, so I force myself to clean my plate. I breathe a quiet sigh of relief when I'm finished, but before I can relax, Mrs. Mahi takes my plate away to refill it.

"No," I plead. "I'm full. Thank you"

"Nonsense," she says, putting more eggplant and rice on my plate. "You can't be full yet. You've hardly eaten."

"Really. I don't eat a lot."

"Don't you like it," she pauses, frowning slightly.

"No. It's wonderful. The food is great."

"Good. Then, here. Eat some more."

Mrs. Mahi reminds me of my Grandmother, who thinks my skinny frame is an insult to her cooking and her good name. Reluctantly, I dig in and manage to force a second helping into my stomach. When she tries to grab my plate a third time, I hold out my hand to stop her.

"I really can't eat anymore," I tell her, "I'm stuffed."

Her lips purse irritably.

"Are you sure," she asks. "There's plenty of food."

"Thank you. I'm really not a big eater. It was wonderful, though."

She glances at Dr. Mahi, then settles into back into her chair.

Next to me, Tarun eats heartily. "The food is so delicious," he says. "I can't stop eating!" Mrs. Mahi smiles brightly, and I realize I could learn to hate Tarun.

When we finish the main meal, she brings out a plate full of gooey, brown squares. "Try some Indian sweets," she says as she puts the food on the table.

I watch the three men grab the morsels. They umm and ah appreciatively. Since I made a fuss about being full, I'm embarrassed to take any, but I can't resist. "I think I can try one," I say, blushing despite myself.

Mrs. Mahi nods her head, and I put one in my mouth. It's like a very sweet jelly, and it's delicious.

"Well, perhaps one more."

Between Tarun, Niranjan and myself, the plate is soon empty. I look up at Mrs. Mahi sheepishly, but she smiles happily at me.

We return to the sitting room once we finish dinner. Dr. Mahi sits in his reclining chair and puts his feet up. Niranjan sits nearest to him on the couch and slouches slightly as if demurring to his superior. Tarun plops forcefully into the middle of the couch, arms out to his sides, filling the space with his confidence and his frame. I sit in the other reclining chair and luxuriate in its soft embrace.

"So," Dr. Mahi begins, nodding in my direction. "Do you think that meditation will spread in the West?"

"I don't know. I think it has spread a little, but I don't really know anyone besides me that meditates. I tried to get my friends and family to try it, but they never did."

"I think spirituality is growing in South Africa," Tarun interjects. "Many people are interested in different things, and yoga and meditation are becoming more popular all the time. I think it's a very progressive country."

"That's very interesting," Dr. Mahi says. "I always imagine other countries follow America's lead. Jason, do you think America is somehow behind other countries in this way? Do you have some idea that you'll maybe use your experiences here, in India, to in some way spread spirituality when you get home?"

"Ha," I laugh and pick nervously at a button by my wrist. "No, I don't think so. I don't see myself as a spiritual leader."

"I intend to get more involved in the spiritual movement in South Africa," Tarun interjects again. "In fact, I met spiritual leaders back home, and one of them invited me to visit a farming village, here in India, that they are sponsoring. I hope that through my modeling, I'll be able to reach many people and perhaps do fundraising for worthy projects. I certainly think the West has a lot to learn from Indian spirituality, and I hope to bring that home with me."

"Very good," Dr. Mahi says. "And I suppose that neither you or Jason are married. Otherwise, you wouldn't be in India. Is this common in the West?"

"I think it is," Tarun responds. "Many people I know try to have careers first, before getting married. Things are complicated back home. It's not so simple like it used to be, where marriages were arranged by our parents and we didn't have to worry about finding a wife. But now, I have to have a career. I have to have money, in order to attract the kind of woman that I want. I need to have success in my career before I can settle down."

"Is it the same for you, Jason? I find this most curious. For us in India, marriage and family are the most important. Career is important, but without marriage, a man isn't a man. In fact, parents pressure their children, push them to meet an arranged spouse and settle down. Don't your parents want you to get married?"

"I think it's more complicated back home," I begin. "I'm sure my parents want me to get married…"

"It's very different in the West," Tarun interrupts. "We also think marriage is important, but it can be very hard to meet the right woman. I know. I've been looking, but I've never found the right one. Who knows? Maybe I'll meet Ms. Right here in India!"

"If that's what you want," Dr. Mahi says, "I think many Indian families will be interested in setting their up daughter with you."

"Do you think so," Tarun blushes.

"Oh, definitely," Niranjan says. "Western men are very desirable."

"So, where do you both think you'll go next, after Nasik?" Dr. Mahi asks.

"I'm not sure," I reply. "I don't really have any plans."

"I'm going to visit that farming village I told you about. Then, I'll go to Mahatma Gandhi's village before ending up in Varanasi!" Tarun exclaims. "I can't wait to see the home of Indian spirituality. I've always wanted to see it, and I can't wait to bathe in the Ganges."

I can feel myself getting angry whenever Tarun jumps into the conversation. I hate that he talks over me, but I can't bring myself to say or do anything about it. It's obvious that Dr. Mahi really wants to hear from me. I think it's because I sat near the front of the meditation hall, which denotes my level of experience relative to the group. I'm flattered by his attention and his implied praise, yet I feel intimidated and am afraid to speak up. What if I ruin his positive impression? I would like to speak more, but as the evening goes on, I simply fall into my habitual, safe, role of listener. At the end of the evening, I know I've missed my only opportunity to really get to know Dr. Mahi. I also missed an opportunity to show off what I know and to express my true feelings. I don't know how they would have responded, but I wish I had had the courage to try.

3.

It's 3:00 AM and I can't sleep. This is unusual because I can generally sleep anytime, anywhere. But not tonight. Niranjan's cousin snores. The cot creaks when I move. It's as hot as a sauna in our little concrete box. My white bed sheets cling tightly to my sweating body. An army of creepy black shadows crawls around the floor. But, what disturbs me the most was my behavior at Dr. Mahi's house. I'm ashamed that I allowed my insecurities to keep me quiet. I came to India to learn a different way of life, yet I have begun my journey by repeating my old mistakes! I hate myself, and my anger keeps me awake.

A few hours later, when the sun's first rays dimly illuminate the room, I'm horrified by what I see. Spiders perch on intricate webs, directly over my bed, slowly dissecting their evening's catch. A line of ants dances a conga along the foot of my bed, carrying bits of garbage for their day's buffet. Fat flies chase each other around the room, practicing aerial combat, and gigantic cockroaches skitter across the floor, doing whatever disgusting things cockroaches do. Tarun, sleeping on a cot to my left, is blissfully ignorant of the bugs which skitter across his bed, and I imagine Niranjan's cousin, snoring peacefully on the other side of the room, is used to this, but now that I see the biodiversity of bugs which surrounds me, I'll never get to sleep.

But there's nowhere to go. I lie feverishly in bed, flitting between sweating to death, being pissed at myself, and feeling paranoid that some errant bug is trying to crawl up my nose, when I hear the creak of the front door opening.

Niranjan steps inside.

"Niranjan," I croak. "Aren't you supposed to be at work today?"

"Yes. But I decided to take the day off so I can be with you guys. I can give you a tour of Nasik if you like. I'm afraid I have to take you on an errand with me first. I'm sorry, it won't take too much time, but there is something I have to do."

We don't mind. Going on an errand is a small price to pay for a native guide. We get up, get dressed, and get the hell out of the bug-infested room.

"Before I show you around Nasik, I want to visit a sannyasin I know and buy some books." Niranjan explains. "Maybe you'll see something you want as well."

"What's a sannyasin?" I ask.

"A sannyasin," Niranjan replies, "is a Hindi holy man who has renounced all his worldly ties, including his family and friends, in order to fully devote himself to spiritual seeking and service of God. This particular man sells religious literature to support himself, and I visit him once in a while to get new books."

We walk down several streets until we reach a large, open, concrete area. Hordes of people jostle each other as they move quickly through the vast space. A large steel cage sits in the middle of the plaza. It's about 24 feet long, 10 feet wide, and 9 feet high. It has large steel bars about two inches in diameter with about four inches of space between them. A large statue and an altar to Hanuman, the monkey god, occupy one half of the cage. The sannyasin, a heavyset Indian man wearing long orange robes, matted, shoulder length hair, and a bushy black beard, lives in the other half. The sannyasin's 'room' contains several piles of books, an ancient metal tape recorder, and a thin mat, which I suppose he sleeps on. These items, along with the robes that he wears and a pair of wire frame glasses, appear to be his only possessions.

It's a very odd combination of seclusion and exposure. On one hand, he lives alone in a cage. On the other hand, the cage sits in the middle of a crowded plaza, where any passerby can look inside and see what he's doing. Judging by the contents of the cage, however, I don't imagine he does anything besides pray, read and sleep.

The sannyasin opens the cage door and smiles warmly at Niranjan, welcoming him inside. Tarun and I climb up after Niranjan and shake the sannyasin's hand. I'm surprised to find that this sedentary, holy man has a very strong grip.

We step into the cage and the metal door clangs shut behind us.

"These are my friends Jason and Tarun. I met them at the meditation retreat I told you about," Niranjan tells the sannyasin. "I want to see what books you have on meditation that might help me in my practice."

The sannyasin nods his head, sorts through his piles of books and picks out a few for Niranjan to peruse. He also hands Niranjan a tape and his antique stainless steel tape recorder. "Listen to this and see what you think," he says.

While the sannyasin speaks with Niranjan, I whisper to Tarun, "this is amazing! Have you ever seen anything like this?"

"Yeah," Tarun says in a flat, heavy voice. "I've seen people like this before. It's all a bunch of nonsense."

I nod my head as I listen, privately annoyed that he's dismissing this experience, but I say nothing. I'm fascinated by this man.

Niranjan sits in a corner of the cage and turns on the tape recorder. The sannyasin turns towards Tarun and me. He smiles warmly and his eyes glow with the light of private mirth.

"Hello," he says in heavily accented English. "Welcome to my home. Please, sit down."

We sit on the metal floor as instructed. The sannyasin puts on a pair of thick reading glasses, opens a book, and begins to read in a deep, resonant voice.

"Our teacher says, 'The human heart can embrace the whole world. All the joys and all the sorrows can find space in the human heart. If you open your heart, you can contain the whole world."

He puts down the book, removes his reading glasses, and looks at us, eyes wide and patient. Tarun stares out the cage, absentmindedly watching the dozens of Indian men and women who pass by, too busy with their daily errands to notice us. But I'm excited to be in the presence of a true ascetic and I'm eager to absorb whatever wisdom he has to offer. I meet the sannyasin's gaze and our eyes lock for a moment before he throws back his bearded head and laughs a huge rumbling laugh that shakes the floor with its force.

Outside, on side of the cage where the idol resides, a man puts money in the offering bowl and rings a bell. He bows deeply to the statue and walks away.

The sannyasin puts his glasses back on, opens his book and resumes his reading.

"Our teacher says, 'You cannot do anything to another that you have not first done to yourself. You cannot harm another person unless you have harmed yourself first. You can not love another person unless you love yourself first.'"

A young woman in a red sari, with a very large red bindi plastered on her forehead, looks up and appears surprised to see me sitting in the cage. She pauses for a brief moment, then returns her gaze to her feet and walks rapidly away. The sannyasin, broad shouldered and hairy, yet so gentle and at ease, looks deeply into my eyes. I ponder what he has read. Before I can attempt to harm another person, I have to get angry at him or her. This unpleasant feeling gnaws at me from the inside, and when I generate this feeling, I effectively harm myself. In the same way, before I can express love for another person, I have to generate a feeling of love inside of me, and, therefore, I get the benefit of this emotion before I share it with another. I think this is what he means, and when I meet his gaze, he laughs his booming, unabashed laughter.

The sannyasin grabs one of my hands with his giant, hairy paw, and turns his attention back to Niranjan. As they discuss Niranjan's books in Hindi, the sannyasin applies pressure to my hand. First he squeezes it, then the pressure lessens. It's a subtle change, and I don't know if it's intentional or not, but when the pattern repeats itself I match his gesture. When he squeezes, I squeeze back. When he loosens his grip, I loosen mine. We do this a few times when, suddenly, he turns his intense black eyes towards me and laughs his earthquake laugh. The cage shakes gently with its' force.

Outside, a man puts a few rupees into the sannyasin's offering bowl, clasps his hands in prayer in front of him, and bows his head reverently. The sannyasin releases my hand, stands up, raises his hand in benediction, and intones a prayer. The Indian man humbly receives the blessing. As soon as it finishes he looks up and shouts at me in Hindi. I watch him, puzzled. What did I do? He glares at me, spits on the ground, and walks away.

"That man has cursed you," the sannyasin translates. "He says that because you're not a Hindu, the gods hate you. He says that you shouldn't even be in this holy land of India."

I can feel the blood rush from my face. This is what I expect. See! My paranoia screams inside my head. They do hate you. They don't want you here. No one wants you. The sannyasin watches me and then laughs again, dispelling my tension.

"The West is hungry," he says. "The East used to have a spiritual hunger, but no more. We have forgotten the meaning of things. But the West is hungry. You are now the seekers."

I can breathe again as I realize that the sannyasin is not upset at me. In fact, he appears to appreciate my eagerness and my sincerity, and has contrasted it positively against the ignorance and hatred of the man who asked for the blessing.

The sannyasin hands me the book he read from and walks over to Niranjan. The book is called *Meditations of the Heart*, written by Osho. Though I don't know much about Indian gurus, I have heard of Osho. During the 80's, Osho was very popular in the United States. He built a great ashram in Oregon and many Americans went there to worship with him. I'm not clear about exactly what happened, but during the next ten years, his popularity dwindled; he was disgraced and, eventually, deported from America. I remember watching an episode of "60 Minutes" which reported that Osho owned a fleet of Rolls Royce cars, ate on golden plates, and generally enjoyed gaudy, expensive material goods.

How is it, I wonder, that a man who has given up almost all his material possessions could be a follower of Osho? Wasn't he ultimately revealed to be a "fake?"

I watch the monk put his arm around Niranjan's shoulders as he patiently speaks to him about the books, and I wonder if the image presented by "60 Minutes," was too simplistic. A guru who is found to love wealth is automatically understood to be a phony. But do human failings necessarily invalidate a teacher's message, or his power to positively affect the lives of his disciples? I know I have always assumed that it does. In fact, I scrutinize so called spiritual teachers, searching for flaws, believing that most of them must be fakes and therefore must have flaws.

As I think about it, I wonder why I demand a teacher be an ideal manifestation of his message before I'll listen to what he has to say. Part of it, I know, is my fear of being brainwashed or hurt. The very term "spiritual guide," contains the implication that someone is "guiding" me to unfamiliar territory. If this person doesn't really know the path to holiness, then I am in danger of being "guided" to a place of harm. How can I know if a teacher is a fake without clues, such as the guru being caught falling victim to the same desires that plague his disciples? In fact, the reason I remember watching this program is because of the great relief I felt when the guru was exposed. I was thankful that "60 Minutes" had kept me safe.

It occurs to me now, however, that part of my relief was feeling that I was safe from being affected by Osho's "spiritual teachings," teachings which might challenge me to change my life. I was glad to be convinced that spiritual teachings were phony, because then I wouldn't have to examine my life or lifestyle, and I wouldn't have to try to change.

Even so, it would have made sense to scrutinize a teacher's lifestyle, because I didn't think I could accept guidance from someone who wasn't enlightened and perfect. But maybe this sannyasin is proof that that's not necessary. Maybe, I can stop searching for the imperfections of others, accept that everyone has failings and simply take in whatever good they have to offer?

The pressure of the sannyasin's gentle gaze recalls me from my reverie. I look up and his soft black eyes are upon me. "Would you like to buy that book?" he asks with a smile.

I'm instantly on my guard. Was he complimenting me just so I'd buy his book? "No thanks," I say quickly.

"Okay." He shrugs slightly and holds out his hand. "Nice to meet you."

I shake his hand firmly. "Thank you for sharing these teachings with us," I say sincerely, trying to relax and meet his kindness.

"Come back anytime," he says. "Anytime."

We step out of the cage and he laughs his rumbling laugh. I feel flattered by his assertion about my Western seeking and ashamed that I was unable to take his kindness in without suspiciously scrutinizing his words and actions. But I know that that's part of the reason I'm here: to learn to accept what people offer me, without filtering it through the prism of my painful past. I want to be open to the goodness and joy of life. I want to learn to be vulnerable, to take risks. And, I remind myself, I am doing that. I just stepped out of a giant cage. I'm on the right path. I just have to keep on going.

4.

Children surround us as we leave the sannyasin's cage.

"One rupee!" they cry. "Some candy," they shout, holding their hands out. I'm on my guard, as usual, but Niranjan doesn't flinch. He puts his hands on their shoulders and softly shoos them away. When they continue to hound us, he smiles and pats them on their heads. He picks them up and throws them into the air. The boys laugh with joy and jump on him, each competing for his attention. He treats them as children rather than beggars, and I'm ashamed at my defensiveness. When they continue to plead for money, despite his efforts to gently decline, he offers them 10 rupees and tells them to share it. They take his money and run away, laughing happily. I'm impressed by the whole episode. It's as if he's demonstrating the very principles I was pondering in the monk's cage – to accept people's goodness without being blind to their flaws. I resolve to try to imitate his actions the next time beggars approach me for money.

Now that his 'errand' is complete, Niranjan offers to take us on a tour of Nasik's holy temples. Since Niranjan didn't bring his car, we have to hire taxis, which becomes a complicated process due to my presence. Taxi drivers routinely refuse to use their meters. Instead, they want to haggle over the price because this assures them of a higher fare. This practice is universally detested, as even local people have to pay inflated prices to travel by taxi. But there is an unspoken price scale. Local people pay a certain price range. Indians from out of town pay a higher price range. Foreigners pay vastly inflated prices. To avoid paying the exorbitant foreigner rate, I have to hide while Niranjan and Tarun (who can pass as a local as long as he doesn't speak) haggle over the price. Once Niranjan and the driver agree on a price, Niranjan calls out to me and I step forward. When I see the look of outrage on the taxi driver's face I feel a rush of satisfaction. He's been tricked into agreeing to drive a foreigner for the local price and I feel like the balance of power has changed. I am no longer the helpless young man who was so easily conned.

Most of the temples we visit are small, cramped, dark and dirty. They all have steps leading up to them, which I assume is so worshipers physically, as well as symbolically, ascend towards holiness. At the top of the stairs is a large bell, which people ring to announce their presence. From there petitioners place fruits and flowers on the temple altar for consumption by the patron deity. These offerings decay quickly because of the heat of the Indian day, so each temple swarms with flies and the unpleasant aroma of rotting food. Pictures of Hindu gods and goddesses adorn the walls. Some have just a few framed paintings, while others are covered in their entirety with pictures and stories, often from the Bhagavad-Gita. And while small temples are generally empty, large temples often support a priest.

The priests have a symbol of their deity painted in gold on their foreheads and wear orange robes.   They want us to make a donation, and in return they will bless us and give us holy water. The first time we see a priest, both Tarun and I are eager to try this. Once the priest gets his donation, he puts a red dot (called a bindi) on our foreheads and gives us some holy water to drink. I try to get into the experience, but it's difficult. Noise, from speeding cars outside or simply from the multitude of Indians clamoring in the neighborhood streets, permeates the temple space. Dozens of people stream in and out constantly, along with the occasional skinny cow. There's no space to be alone. No place for quiet contemplation. The bindi feels slimy and itchy on my forehead. The water has an unpleasant metallic taste to it. Despite my resolve to drop my judging mind and soak in what is being offered, I can't do it. After the first attempt, I stop giving donations as I don't want either the dot or the water. Priests begin to curse me, angry that the foreigner is refusing to give a donation, and I learn to stay outside while Tarun and Niranjan enjoy the day. The whole experience kind of sucks, which is depressing because I was looking forward to getting a true sense of Indian life and spirituality.

I resolve to be patient and bite my tongue as I know that Tarun is enjoying his entrée into Hinduism, but after two hours I've had about as much as I can take.

"Niranjan," I say.

"Yes."

"Are there other sites to see, besides all these temples?"

"Yes, of course. But, I had wanted to take you to at least one other place."

"Oh…all right."

"Jason?"

"Yes."

"Are you not enjoying this?"

"Well, not really. I'm sorry. I'm having trouble connecting with what I'm seeing. It's very different from what I'm used to. And it's hard to focus on spirituality when it's so dirty and noisy and there are these starving cows everywhere."

"What do you know about reincarnation?" Niranjan asks me seriously.

"Um. Not a lot, I guess. As I understand it, our actions generate something called Karma. If I do something good, then I generate good Karma, and if I do something bad, then I generate bad Karma. When I die, then the accumulation of this Karma will determine what my next life is like."

"Yes. That's very good. You understand a lot, but let me explain it a bit more. We believe that there is a hierarchy of life in which some life forms are more blessed than others. In the animal kingdom, for example, there are human beings, cows, dogs, cats, mice, etc. What kind of actions we performed in our previous lives, good or bad, determine our next incarnation, whether we become an evolved being with a happy life, like a rich human being with a large family, or a lower being with a difficult life, like an abused dog.

"Near the top of this hierarchy is man, the most blessed of all animals. That the three of us have all been incarnated as men shows that we had a lot of past good Karma. Next in line to men are cows. They are just below humans in the hierarchy of life.

"Look," he points to a skinny white cow standing by the side of the road. "Look in its eyes. They have human eyes."

Tarun and I pause to look. The cow, so emaciated that its ribs are clearly visible beneath its dirty white hide, stares at us with giant brown human eyes. It's creepy. Suddenly I feel like all my life, cows have been watching me, and I never knew it.

"Since human beings are considered to be sacred," Niranjan continues, pleased by our shocked expressions, "so are cows. For this reason, no Hindu is allowed to harm a cow.

"However, if you want to be a bit more rational about it, some people believe that we consider cows to be sacred because our ancestors were farmers. Farmers rely on cows for two essential life-giving ingredients: milk and dung. Milk feeds and sustains the farmer's family, providing nutrients they could not live without, and dung is blessed with two properties, both essential to the poor farmer. The first is the fact that dung contains gas, which allows farmers to use it to light fires for cooking and warmth. Once the gas is consumed, the dung is used as fertilizer. Therefore, people say, cows are considered to be sacred in India because they provide farmers, with sustenance, nutrition, warmth, and fertilizer."

"But, there is a much more important reason, I think," Niranjan continues. "My teacher, the man we met earlier today, taught me this. He says that Hinduism teaches us to revere cows because cows are a living example of the holy trait of selfless giving, and in India, selfless giving is an ideal way of life."

"What are you talking about?" I interject. "How can cows be an example of selfless giving? All they do is lounge around all day and eat grass."

"Ah," Niranjan replies. "That's how it looks to you, but you are a city person. Tell me, before you came here, had you ever seen cows close up?"

"No. Not really."

"So, you don't really know anything about cows?"

"Well, no, I guess not," I admit, as I step over a large pile of decaying shit, momentarily forcing the feasting flies to flee.

"Then think about this," Niranjan points his finger at me for emphasis. "A female cow gives the farmer all the fruits of her body, her milk and her dung. In return for these life sustaining products, created from the hard work of her body, the selfless cow asks for nothing. She simply goes out to pasture and eats some grass. Similarly, a bullock, a male cow, will work hard all day for the farmer, pulling his cart, plowing his field, and in return for a hard day's grueling work the cow asks for nothing, but simply goes out to pasture and eats some grass. In both instances, cows give everything they have to give, all for the benefit for the farmer, and in return ask only that they be allowed to do what they need to do to survive. Cows are a symbol of selfless giving."

"Huh," I mutter. "I'll have to think about that."

"Hinduism is one of the world's oldest religions," Niranjan reminds me. "There is great wisdom and great holiness in its practices and its teachings. Try to be open to it. I think you will find a way to connect to what it has to offer.

"I have an idea," he says suddenly. "Will you allow me to take you to one more temple?"

"Of course. I'm sorry I complained."

"Don't worry about it. I just want to give you both a sense of what Hinduism has to offer. Let's try just one more."

We take a taxi to our final temple. I tell myself to be open to the experience, but I'm tired. I don't think I have the energy for any more Hindu spirituality. As we walk into the courtyard, however, I feel my breath catch in my throat. Over the noise of the multitude of people we're wading through, I hear a scream of joy – a brazen full-throated roar like nothing I've ever heard. My inner critic shuts up. What the heck is this?

We follow the sound to a small platform. There, a few musicians play a lilting, melodic rhythm while a woman stands between them, her body swaying to the music. Her voice accompanies the music, but every so often it rises above it in a loud shout of joy, which seems to originate in her belly and shake her entire body as it erupts from her throat. I can feel it pierce me: my feet are rooted to the spot. I've never heard anything so vibrantly alive. We all watch, breathless, as the woman pours out her passion, her full-bodied conviction, her joy. The music and her voice send shivers of electricity through my spine...until, suddenly, the song ends, and silence hides the emptiness that remains. The woman opens her eyes, smiles, and turns away.

"This is called Bhajans," Niranjan explains as he leads us back to the street. "In this form of worship a devotee attempts to completely submerse herself in song, until her identity becomes so fused with the singing that she becomes one with her god and is no longer aware of her own existence, becoming literally without self.

"This," he confides to us, "is the form of worship I'd like my wife to follow. Meditation is for men. It's too difficult, too intellectual for women. But this is a feminine form of worship. It's about devotion, not intellect."

Though I am profoundly moved by what I have just heard, I disagree. For me, meditation was the answer to my unspoken prayers, the secret to healing hidden wounds. I think everyone should experience it.

"That was amazing." I tell him, "and it would be wonderful if your wife wanted to do that, but there's no reason she couldn't try meditation too. The philosophy of meditation isn't important," I continue, feeling that as a more experienced meditator I can lecture him about it. "It's intended to enhance and support the meditation, but it's not essential that someone be smart and understand fine points of philosophy to do the work of meditation. If your wife were interested in taking a meditation course, I think that would be great. It's certainly not just for men."

Niranjan shakes his head in disagreement. He grabs our hands, and we quickly run across the street, dodging between speeding cars.

"Meditation," he continues once we safely reach the other side, "my chosen form of worship, is for men. My wife should do something different."

"Why do you say that? Have you spoken to her about it? What did she think of your experience?"

"Well…it's a bit complicated."

"What do you mean?"

"My wife didn't really want me to go. Our marriage has been a bit difficult."

Niranjan looks down at his shoes, clearly embarrassed, and I realize I have blundered into a sensitive topic.

"I'm sorry," I say quickly. I wish now I'd just kept my mouth shut.

"Look," he says. "A few years ago I met my true love. And, she loved me. We wanted to get married, but India is a very conservative society. In general, parents arrange marriages for their children. Even in a case such as ours, what is called a 'love match,' it is understood that we would need our parents' consent.

"I went to Sujata's house and spoke with her parents many times, begged them to allow me to marry her. Her father refused. He said he was sorry, but my caste was too low, and I didn't make enough money. 'Look around you,' he said. 'Look at what I have provided for my daughter. Be honest.' He said. 'Could you do the same?' I knew that I couldn't, but for a year I pleaded with him. I tried to show him how hard I worked. I told him how much I loved his daughter. It didn't matter. Sujata also implored him, but that didn't matter either. I would never be what Sujata's father wanted for his daughter. I would never be able to win his approval.

"Sujata asked me to elope with her. She didn't care what her parents thought. She wanted to marry me. But I couldn't do it that way. I don't know if you can understand, but without a traditional wedding, done with our parents' approval, we would have lost everything. Our families would no longer speak to us. Even our friends would have shunned us. We would have had to move to another town where no one knew us and start over. Even so, Sujata was willing. But I couldn't."

"Why not?" I ask.

"My parents need me. They live with me. I pay the rent and buy the food. Plus, I'm supporting my sister's family. They all rely on the money I make from my job."

"I don't understand. It sounds like they couldn't afford to shun you."

"That's it," he says. "But, if I eloped or married a girl without her family's permission, they would have had to stop speaking to me. There's enormous social pressure. I don't know how they could have survived. I couldn't do this to them. I begged Sujata to be patient. I would convince her father." He pauses for a moment, and I look away, embarrassed and humbled by his pain.

"Sujata gave up on me," he continues. "She loved me, but I wouldn't marry her without her father's permission, and she couldn't wait forever. She allowed her father to find her a husband. She married someone else."

Niranjan is quiet for a moment, then he continues. "A few years later, my mother started insisting I let her find me a bride. I refused. I didn't want anyone else, but she persisted. Just to get her to stop, I agreed to see the woman she had picked. When I saw the woman, and still said no, my mother started to cry. It went on and on for days, and I couldn't stand it. Eventually, I agreed. We were married a month ago. It's very hard. I'm trying to learn to love her…she's really very beautiful…she tries to please me, but it's hard."

Niranjan's pain is palpable. Around us, vendors, selling fruits and nuts call out for our attention. An elderly beggar looks up from the curb and holds out a paper cup in his shaking hand. We walk between and among the ubiquitous hustle and bustle of street traffic, quietly subdued by the tragedy of Niranjan's life story. I'd like to say something to help alleviate his pain, but what can I offer? I am a single man, with little dating experience. I've never been in love. I'm not really sure I'd know it if I found it.

I feel torn and confused. My parents often pressure me to make the kinds of decisions that they want me to make. I resist with every fiber of my being because it would feel like some sort of soul-suicide if I lived my life according to their dictates. But perhaps I am a selfish man. No one relies on me like Niranjan's parents rely on him. I can see that what he did was noble. He gave up what he wanted in order to help his family. And now he has to learn to live with his decisions, with his life. And he has to do it by himself. He obviously can't talk to his parents or his bride about how he feels. Maybe he can't talk to his friends either.

This, I realize, is why Niranjan took the meditation course. He's taking the time he needs to try to recover from a broken heart and find the strength to love anew. He found people he could be with who wouldn't judge him, and we're with him for the same reason. We all want to find our way to happiness and fulfillment, and we all need time away from friends and family to understand what this could be for us. I put my arm around his shoulder, hoping that my friendship and silent support will be as helpful to him as his kindness is for me.

5.

"I can't wait for you to meet my wife," Niranjan drives onto a dirt lot behind two squat, white concrete, apartment complexes, and parks his car. "She's excited to meet you. My parents will be there as well."

We leave the small blue car and approach a large metal door, which squeaks loudly as Niranjan pulls it open. We climb a concrete stairway, and as we do, people open their doorways, greet Niranjan and unabashedly stare at us. Niranjan introduces us to everyone, and it seems as though the whole building has been foretold of our arrival.

Niranjan's apartment door opens immediately after he knocks, and his wife stands before us, wearing a beautiful red sari interlaced with rushing gold swirls. Next to her is his mother, wearing a shimmering, light, powder blue sari. Niranjan's father hovers behind the two women, wearing simple tan cotton pants and a button down shirt.

Niranjan's wife, a petite, thin, pretty woman, steps forward to meet me as I step through the open doorway. Her golden nose ring sparkles in the room's pale light. I hold out my hand to shake hers, but she eludes my outstretched arm, bows before me, crosses her arms and touches my feet. I tense up and can feel the heat rising to my face. What is the appropriate response to your hostess bowing and touching your feet?

She rises gracefully and steps towards Tarun. He puts his hands gently on her shoulders, as he doesn't want her to bow to him, but she lightly steps out of his grasp and bows and touches his feet. Now we both stand awkwardly.

Niranjan's happy voice rings out from behind us.

"This is a traditional Hindu welcome. My wife bids our honored guests to enter and feel at home."

Tarun and I walk towards her, thinking we should return the gesture, but she frantically evades us. We chase her for a brief moment, then stop, as it's clear that she really doesn't want us to bow to her. Now what?

Niranjan's father, a very small, skinny man, steps forwards and shakes our hands. Niranjan's mother, a heavyset woman, nods politely at us.

"Please come in," Niranjan says. "Here. Sit down."

He indicates that we should sit on the room's only piece of furniture: an old grey couch. It sags heavily in the middle, and has holes and exposed padding throughout. Opposite the couch is a small television set, which is the only other item in the room besides a few small lamps. Insects scurry in between the pieces of furiously peeling blue paint which vainly tries to cover the walls.

As we sit down, Niranjan's wife hurries out of the room. He glances at his mother, who says, "Tvari has gone to the kitchen to check on the food."

"My wife is very shy," Niranjan adds. "I know she's excited to meet you. But, she's a bit afraid."

Niranjan turns to his mother. "Could you go and ask her to join us, please."

Niranjan's mother rises slowly, her back straight, her chin high, as if she's going out on an important mission. When she returns, she smiles and shrugs her shoulders.

"Tvari is too busy to come out right now." She explains.

"That's too bad," Tarun says loudly. "I was really hoping to get a chance to talk to her."

"Niranjan," I say, raising my voice as well. "Your wife was so gracious. I hope she will finish working and can join us soon."

We allow a respectful period of silence to follow our blatant attempts to draw her out, but she remains with the food where she's safe.

Niranjan's father turns to me. "What do you do in America and how much do you make?"

"He's not being rude," Niranjan interjects quickly. "In India questions about money are common and are not considered to be private matters."

He turns to his father. "In America such questions *are* considered to be rude. You shouldn't ask him such things."

"It's okay," I assure Niranjan. "I don't mind."

I turn to Niranjan's father. "Before I came to India, I was working in New York City as an English language teacher. I was making about $15 per hour, which came to $450 per week."

"And how much is that in rupees?"

"Well…it's 40 rupees for one dollar, so it comes to about 600 rupees per hour."

Niranjan's father whistles in astonishment. "600 rupees per hour! I never heard of someone making so much money!"

"Yeah, but it's not equivalent to what that money is worth here" I say quickly. "In America, what I made was a very small salary. My rent was $1,000 per month. I barely made enough to pay my bills…"

Niranjan's father isn't listening to me anymore. "600 rupees per hour. Not a large salary? Amazing! All Americans really are rich!"

He looks at me sharply. "Are you married?"

"No."

"Why not?"

"Dad!" Niranjan interjects. "Please. You're being rude."

"I'm just asking a simple question."

"But he may not want to answer all these personal questions."

Niranjan turns to look at us. "Would you guys like to watch some TV? We have cable."

"Yeah. Do you get CNN?" I ask, taking advantage of the diversion. "I haven't seen the news for two weeks now."

"Sure." Niranjan turns on the TV, and I sink into the couch and try to hide. I felt like I was enduring a college interview about my personal life, and I'm relieved to have it over. The truth is I've only had two relationships. Both were with women who were dependent on me.

Neither took care of my needs. I have come to understand that this was largely my fault. Because I didn't feel that I had anything to offer them, I felt unworthy of their care and affection, and I insisted on taking care of them. This helped offset my own insecurities, but led to the development of relationships where I was never happy. It also led me to choose women who would allow such one-sided giving. I believe that this will continue to happen as long as I feel ashamed about who I am, and so I've stopped trying to date. Along with finding a career path, I hope that coming to India will help me know myself better, value my skills and virtues more fully, so I can gain enough confidence to have a healthy relationship with another person. I know that I can't be as bad as I feel I am, but I don't know how to change how I feel.

So, the honest answer to Niranjan's father's question is, I'm not married because I'm not ready to be married. And I'm not sure I ever will be. I could, of course, share my feelings and fears. Though I want to experiment with revealing my true self, I'm too frightened. I'm afraid that they wouldn't understand, and I'm afraid of being judged.

We watch coverage of the President Clinton/Monica Lewinsky scandal until Niranjan's mother tells him that dinner is ready.

"We have to decide where we want to eat," Niranjan says.

The apartment is very small. It has the living room we've been sitting in, a small kitchen, one bedroom (shared jointly by Niranjan, his wife, and his parents), and its one main luxury: a small wooden deck, which is about six feet wide and five feet long.

"We can eat in here. It's crowded, but there are fewer bugs. On the other hand, we can eat outside on the deck."

Niranjan, I discover, doesn't own any chairs or tables, so either way we'll have to sit on the floor. As there's more room outside, and it's less stuffy, we decide to eat there.

Niranjan's wife brings out cans of soda, a special luxury reserved for honored guests, and plate upon plate of vegetables, fried bread, and white rice.

"We know that Americans don't like food as spicy as we like it," Niranjan's mother tells us. "So, we tried to minimize this. Let us know what you think."

It's not terribly spicy. Unfortunately, the vegetables are all so oily or greasy or fried that my stomach feels queasy. Even so, I force myself to eat. "It's great," I mumble between mouthfuls.

I want to compliment Niranjan's wife, but it's impossible to slow her down. If someone finishes their soda, she gets them another. If a dish is empty, she runs into the kitchen to refill it. She's a constant blur of motion.

"Tvari," I say gently, as she comes to refill my plate for a third time. "I really can't eat any more. I hope you are not too busy to eat yourself."

"I've already had my dinner," she stares at the ground as she speaks, avoiding my eyes. "Let me get you some more."

"No. Please don't…" It's too late. She snatches away my plate and hurries back to the kitchen.

My hostesses routinely ignore my attempts to stop eating and I wonder, in India, if hungry people routinely refuse extra helpings of food, even if they want more, to protect the host family from too much financial strain. The problem is that I actually mean it when I say I'm full.

My butt and legs begin to feel sore. I'm not used to sitting on a hard floor for extended periods of time, and I fidget and have to change positions every few minutes. For the first time in my life I realize furniture and silverware are luxuries that some people can't afford.

Niranjan's family cringes whenever I shift positions, but there is nothing anyone can do about it. They can't offer me furniture they don't have, and I can't suddenly get used to sitting on a wooden floor for hours at a time.

Several of Niranjan's friends stop by during the meal and by the time we finish eating, the deck is crowded. They all dream of coming to America, where they believe they could get a job, make a lot of money and have all the things that people on TV have. Everyone wants to know if this is true. Are all Americans wealthy? Do they all have TVs? Do they eat in restaurants every night?

"I don't think it's that different from anywhere else," I explain. "How much money you make depends on what kinds of skills you have and what job you get. Some people probably eat out every night, but most don't. Most people do have TVs, however."

"I agree," Tarun interjects. "Life in the West is not like what you see on TV. I don't know what it's like in America, but in South Africa there are both rich and poor people. It's not so easy to make money like you think"

Niranjan's friends listen politely, but when Tarun finishes speaking, they immediately return their attention to me. I feel sorry for Tarun. Despite his Indian ancestry and his exciting career, Niranjan's family and friends are primarily interested in learning about America.

"How much do factory workers make?" one of them asks me.

"I don't know. Probably not very much, though."

This stops the flow of conversation for a moment. They are Niranjan's friends, so they are probably all factory workers.

"But how much approximately?" the man asks again.

"I really don't know. I'm sorry, I don't know any factory workers at home. I couldn't even guess. But you have to remember. If you're in America, it's an expensive place to live. Even though an American job will pay you more money than you'd get here, probably a lot more, you have to pay rent and for food and transportation, which would also cost a lot more."

"But if we could save just a little, we could send the money home to our families here and it would help a lot."

"Yeah. That's probably true," I admit.

"How much did your plane ticket cost?"

"1,000 dollars for a round trip ticket."

"How much is that in rupees?"

"About 40,000."

A heavy silence follows this pronouncement. "We only make about 10,000 rupees a year," Niranjan says. The other men shake their heads.

"How many years would it take us to save that much?" he asks his friends rhetorically.

"What about getting a visa?" one of them asks me. "I hear that's almost impossible."

"I don't know."

"I know someone who said it takes many years."

"Perhaps Canada offers us a better chance," Niranjan says wistfully. But by looking at their glum faces, I can see that this too is probably an impossible dream.

As with any relationship, I feel I need to do something to repay them for being kind to me. I imagine telling them that I'll sponsor them. I could let them stay with me rent free while they work and support their families. But, I don't actually make this offer because I don't want to take on that kind of responsibility. And, because I don't offer to help them, I feel guilty. In my imagination, they invited me over so I could help them achieve their dreams, and I fear that if I don't, they'll be upset with me.

Instead, they frown and hang their heads when Niranjan announces that he's going to take us home, and when I get up to leave, each person shakes my hand with a firm grip and thanks me for coming with a quiver in their voice I can't deny. They actually enjoyed meeting me! I try to soak this in. They were grateful for the company and the conversation, just as I am. Maybe, if I can let my guard down, I'll find that people can appreciate me simply for who I am. And that, I think, could change everything.

6.

The next day I pay the price for Niranjan's hospitality. When I wake, I'm instantly aware of an awful pain in my stomach. I have to go to the bathroom and I have to go right now! I grab a few pieces of toilet paper and race out of the door. The rocks on the ground hurt my bare feet but I can't pause to consider where I step. I don't even have time to shut the bathroom door behind me. I'm barely able to get my pants down before a torrential flood of liquid shoots out of my body. I squat over the smelly hole, feeling drained and sick. My whole body aches. Suddenly, I have to throw up, and I whirl around and vomit into the pit of my own waste. I wash the floor with a bucket of water and, bent over like an old man suffering from arthritis, creep back to the room.

Over the next hour I have to repeat this process three times. My stomach aches horribly, and my butt hurts. When I return the third time, Tarun is awake.

"Are you all right?" he asks.

"No. I feel awful. All I want to do is lie down and be close to a bathroom."

"Do you think you got sick from the food?"

"Yeah," I wince. "How do you feel?"

"I feel fine," he says.

I hate him when he gets out of bed, stretches, yawns, and gets dressed like a healthy person. Why didn't the food make him sick too?

"There's a pharmacy just down the street," he says. "I'll get you some electrolyte powder and some water. If you're throwing up, you'll need it to keep from getting dehydrated."

"Thank you," I mutter, feeling guilty for wishing he was sick.

He's gone for only a few minutes. When he returns, he has the promised water and powder.

"I bought you some bread too. You should be able to keep that down, if you can keep anything down."

"Thank you."

Tarun starts to look through his guidebook, searching for something he can do alone, when there's a knock at the door. He answers it, and Niranjan enters.

"Hi," Tarun says. "Aren't you supposed to be at work today?"

"Yes, but I decided to take the day off so I can be with you again. Are you all right?" he asks me. "You look terrible."

"I feel sick."

"Oh, no. It's not the food, is it? My wife made sure not to make it too spicy."

"No," I reassure him. "It's not your fault. Look, Tarun feels fine, and he ate the same food. Please don't tell your wife I got sick. I don't want her to feel bad."

"Well, okay. I thought I'd take you guys to the source of the Godavari River. Do you think you can come with us?"

"No. Thank you. I need to be close to a bathroom."

"Tarun, what do you think?"

"Sure. Let's go."

"We'll back in a few hours. Do you need anything?"

"No. Tarun has taken good care of me. I'll see you guys when you get back. Have fun."

I'm sorry I can't go with them, but I'm also relieved when they are gone. Puking is a solitary business.

7.

The next day marks our final morning in Nasik. Tarun asked me if I wanted to accompany him on his travels, and I said yes. I have no agenda of my own, and going with him beats traveling by myself again. Though my stomach is still upset and I feel weak and sore, I'm well enough to travel. As much as I've enjoyed Niranjan's hospitality, I'm ready to go.

I'm supposed to be packing and getting ready, but instead I'm lying in bed, feeling tired and sick, waiting for Tarun to return from last minute shopping, when Niranjan bursts through the apartment door.

"We have to go," he says, picking up Tarun's packed bag. "Now." He says, seeing my confused, deer in headlights look. "We have to go meet Tarun and your train leaves in fifteen minutes!"

I throw my clothes into my bag and we run outside. Niranjan climbs aboard a motorcycle. "Get on," he says.

I stand next to him, stupefied.

My bag is four and a half feet long and very heavy. Riding motorcycles even under good conditions, terrifies me. Riding a motorcycle on the chaotic, pothole strewn, animal-clogged, congested Indian streets seems suicidal. Negotiating this insanity with a seventy-pound bag on my lap…

"Don't worry," Niranjan says. "I'll go slow."

The only way to get the backpack and myself onto the motorcycle's small seat is to put it sideways on my lap. In this position it sticks out a foot and a half on either side like bulky, fat, black wings. Niranjan said he would go slow, but the moment I'm aboard he guns the engine, and we fly down the street. People, cows, cars, dogs, and potholes pass by in an insane blur. He has to keep yelling at people and honking his horn in order to give them enough time to lunge aside as we zip by. Since the bag is behind Niranjan, I wonder how he's able to judge our ability to squeeze between cars or fit in narrow, dank alleyways. We miss several buildings and people by very thin margins. Each pothole we hit launches me into the air. The balancing act of holding onto both Niranjan's back and my bulky pack gives me something to focus on, something over which I might have some control. I hug the motorcycle with my knees like I'm riding a horse, which doesn't exactly give me a good grip. At any moment I'm sure I'm going to fall off. My brains will be splattered on the dirty asphalt. I'll never see my family again…

We turn a corner, and I see Tarun and Niranjan's mother, standing calmly in front of a store. Niranjan pulls over to the side and I stumble off in my haste to disembark. Niranjan parks his bike and runs into the street to hail a taxi.

Tarun beams happily. "Look at what I got," he says. I look at his purchases and can only nod mutely in approval. Two beautiful saris: soft, supple, and delicately designed. I've never seen clothing so gorgeous, and I resolve to purchase some for my loved ones before I return home.

Niranjan runs back from the street with tears in his eyes.

"The taxi's waiting. He'll take you to the station" he says. "Don't forget me," he pleads, as he hugs us both.

I feel a lump settle in my throat. I don't know too many men capable of honestly revealing themselves and being as vulnerable as he was, and not many people in my life have been as generous with their home and with their time.

As I wave goodbye to him, I remember his story of how cows symbolize selfless giving and how Hindus aspire to embody this sacred trait. Whereas I had suspected Niranjan's motives, he never suspected mine. He wanted to befriend me. He wanted to share his life with me. And in return, he simply wanted my friendship. I'm fortunate that I was forced to accept his generosity. I hope that during this trip I can learn to be as open and giving as Niranjan.

8.

Tarun and I are two innocents who have yet to be baptized in the ordeal of Indian train travel. When we walk into the station we are lost. All we know is that our train is supposed to arrive soon. We think, being naïve foreigners, that the man at the Enquiry window will tell us where to go, but we soon learn the first lesson of Indian train travel: trying to discover which platform a train will arrive on is like trying to get the government to discuss classified information. "Your train usually arrives on platform two or six," is all the man at the window will tell us. As to the time of its arrival or departure, he will go as far as to confirm what the schedule says, but he warns us that this is only a vague guideline. What we need to do, he says, is "wait at platform two until you are hearing the announcement for your train. At that time, you will know which is the correct platform where the train is going to stop."

To get from platform two to six we would have to climb a flight of black, metal stairs, walk across an overhead walkway, and descend another flight of stairs. I believe if I ran at full speed I could run up the stairs and across the walkway in about 30 seconds. With my giant duffel bag stuffed with American 'necessities,' it would take a lot longer. It's not hard to guess that the train might not stay more than a minute or two. I can envision Tarun, with his light pack and his athlete's body, running nimbly across the walkway and jumping on the train as it pulls away, while I struggle to lug my bag up the first flight of stairs. It's an unhappy thought, but I'm spared when the crackly PA system announces that our train will indeed arrive on platform two.

It is at this time that we learn the second important lesson of Indian train travel: When the PA system announces the arrival of a train, run for your life. The station instantly swarms with the seething motion of frenetic families scrambling to grab their luggage and children, desperate to get to the announced track and find their berth as quickly as possible. Footsteps pound the ground. The smell of burning metal wafts through the station, as a faint gray smoke fills the air. Tarun and I are helplessly carried along, filled with an urgent feeling of panic, terrified because we don't know where we're going and we don't know what we're going to do when we get there. What we do know is that if Indians, who we presume have done this before, are panicking, then ignorant foreigners should panic as well.

As we run around the platform in a state of near hysteria, we learn another lesson of Indian train travel: although our tickets conveniently list the number of the car our seats are in, the number rarely appears on the car itself. Someone is supposed to paste numbers on the cars before the train leaves the first station, but this is not always done. In addition, the numbers don't seem to run sequentially, so finding one car with a number on it (if it's not our number) doesn't help us figure out which car contains our seats. We are lost in the midst of hundreds of running, pushing, shoving, desperate people, overwhelmed by the noise of yelling, train breaks squealing, and our pulses pounding.

Porters, skinny men in faded red suits carrying luggage on their heads, roughly shoulder us aside. They seem to know exactly where they're going, and their lucky employers scurry behind them, safe and sure of boarding the train on time. Those of us without porters are in deep shit.

Tarun and I pick up our bags and try to ask people to look at our tickets and tell us where to go. Most are in too much of a hurry to even notice we're trying to speak to them. A porter recognizes us as foreigners and directs us to the first class car. He doesn't wait long enough for me to explain that we bought second-class tickets. We stick our heads into open train windows and ask people for car S4. They point in one direction, and we run that way. We ask some other people, and they point in the opposite direction. We turn around and run some more. Because I'm lagging behind, panting like an exhausted dog, Tarun takes my large bag from my hands, and I take his smaller one. After a few minutes of frantic searching the train begins to depart without us. We grab hold of the nearest doorway and pull ourselves aboard. From here we have no choice but to pick a direction and walk through the train compartments in search of the elusive S4.

By the time we find our beds, we're exhausted. I look around expecting to see a relieved look on everyone's face, but people sit calmly on their seats as if nothing unusual occurred. After a moment of shame and shock, I realize that nothing special has happened. That explosion of panic and chaos is simply what people do when boarding a train at a busy station.

I survey the train, wondering what else passes for normal here. Each car is divided into narrow rectangular compartments, enclosing eight beds: three each on the long sides, one above the other, and two on the narrow side, also one above the other. The compartment is without doors, so no one has any privacy. Three people can sit comfortably on the lower beds and there is adequate room for one person to lie down on each bed. Unfortunately, comfort is a rare commodity in India. Not only do two people commonly sleep on the same bed, but four or five people generally sit on the lower beds during the day. In addition, many people ride the Indian trains without paying for a bed. These people lay a thin sheet on the ground and sleep on the floor. At night, to get up and go to the bathroom means stepping over sleeping people. In the darkness, with the uneven rocking motion of the train, it's a minefield.

The people around us ask where we're going, where we're from and what we do, but their curiosity is quickly sated, and they soon ignore us. Tarun and I, sharing the top, thinly padded metal slab that is my bunk bead, play gin rummy. Below us, other passengers eat food, talk tiredly, or simply rest on the cushions.

During our card game I consider going to the bathroom, but fear makes me cautious. After using Niranjan's outhouse and after seeing the decrepit condition of the train station and the trains, I'm afraid to investigate the train's bathroom. I make a firm and final decision to avoid the bathroom at all costs when an unbearably potent smell of urine and feces wafts through the train. It's so vile, I gag. I don't care if my bladder explodes. I can wait! From the smell I imagine that the bathroom is simply a room where people defecate. No toilet. No toilet paper. No hole. Just a room full of fresh shit. Unless I think I'm going to die, I'm not going in there!

After several hours, I'm in a great deal of pain, but that smell is fresh in my memory. I use all my willpower and clamp down on my urgent need. It's 10:00 in the evening. We're supposed to arrive at 6:00 a.m. I figure if I can just get to sleep, when I wake up we'll be there.

Tarun shakes me roughly until I open my eyes.

"We're here," he says. "Hurry. We're an hour and a half early. Those people remembered where we were going. We're lucky they woke me."

I rub my eyes, sit up, and instantly feel the worst pain I have ever felt in my life. It's centered in my abdomen, but it knifes through my whole body. I have to go to the bathroom immediately! It doesn't matter that we're at my station. It doesn't matter what the condition of the bathroom is. I have to go! But I can't move. I've consumed nothing but liquids for the past day because I've been afraid I couldn't keep anything else down. Now everything I drank rushes past my defenses. I grab my towel and stick it down my pants, hoping I can create a makeshift diaper. The good news is that my towel absorbs most of it. The bad news is I don't smell very good and my pants are wet. I untuck my shirt and cover the mess.

I put my towel in a large Ziploc bag I have and hope no one noticed what happened to me. In the commotion of the train's arrival, no one has. Tarun and I get off the train. I feel ashamed. I should have simply faced my pain and fear and gone to the bathroom, instead of waiting until necessity stole choice from me, but at least I'm not in pain anymore. The sickness is over now. It's time to face India anew.

Varanasi

After leaving Nasik, we spent a few days at a farming village, learning how a group from South Africa is trying to help the farmers keep their traditions and their land, despite the pressures to sell their assets and move to the city. From there, we visited Sevagram, a village Mahatma Gandhi founded, which still lives according to his vision of how India could achieve peace and prosperity, without being beholden to foreign influence. Now, two weeks later, we've arrived at Varanasi.

I've enjoyed our trip so far, and though I haven't found the key to personal happiness, I do feel more comfortable getting around India – even if the biggest success I've had so far is getting on and off the right train. But, I'm starting to get restless. While it is fun to meander through Indian cities, I have a higher purpose, and I'm on the alert for a signal, either internal or external, which will indicate where I need to go and what I need to do.

We disembark from our train and exit the station. In front of us lies a gray, paved lot about 50 feet long. Rows of yellow taxis sit idly in neat rows, as their drivers huddle together, swapping stories and passing the time. It's 6:00 AM and we are the only tourists looking for a ride. As we walk towards the parking area, we approach a young man sitting on the curb. He looks up at us as we pass.

"You need a taxi?"

"Yes," I say. "How much to the Dasaswamedh Ghats?"

"25 rupees," he says.

Tarun and I look at each other. I asked a tourist officer in the train station what the ride should cost, and he advised us to pay 20 rupees, so it's tempting.

"You should trust me," he says, pushing his thick spectacles up the bridge of his nose. "It's a fair price."

This makes up my mind. If I've learned nothing else during my time in India, it's that I should never trust a taxi driver. I shake my head no to Tarun.

We walk into the rickshaw parking area, and taxi drivers surround us. The first man we speak to us wants 30 rupees. So does the next and the next. Soon, the whole crowd is shouting.

"30 rupees."

"Right this way."

"In here sir."

"Follow me."

It's clear that 25 rupees is as good as it's going to get. We make our way back to the man with the thick glasses.

"Okay." Tarun says. "We'll go with you."

The young man blinks at us. Then he shakes his head no.

"30 rupees," he says.

Tarun starts to lose his cool.

"You said 25 rupees."

The man shakes his head again.

"30 rupees. You should have trusted me."

Tarun takes a step forward, towering over the seated man.

"You said 25. You'll take us for 25!"

I'm afraid he's about to provoke a physical confrontation, but the little guy knows who's in charge.

"Okay." He says calmly. "35 rupees."

We look at him in disbelief. What kind of haggling ploy is this?

The man turns and nods to the crowd of drivers.

They smile and shout, "35 rupees! 35 rupees!"

We whirl around, confused by the barrage of prices. Then, a voice shouts, "40 rupees!"

And suddenly all the drivers yell, "40 rupees! 40 rupees!"

This is getting out of hand. Desperate, we turn back towards the seated man. He looks at us for a moment.

"45 rupees," he says, quietly.

The crowd roars its delight and begins to chant the new price.

Tarun's face turns red. He storms over to one of the men in the crowd and towers over him. He's about twice the size of this man, and he jabs his finger into the man's shoulder.

"Take us for 25 rupees!"

Again, I'm afraid Tarun's about to start a fight, but, surprisingly, the rickshaw wallah nods his head in agreement and motions for us to get into his taxi. Tarun looks at me and smiles smugly.

I don't know why that worked, but I'm not going to argue. I put my backpack into the back seat, squeeze in next to it and sigh, thinking we've somehow gotten the last laugh.

The driver gets in, turns around to look at us, and grins broadly.

"25 rupees each," he says. All around us, we can hear the other drivers laughing and shouting, "50 rupees! 50 rupees!"

I trip over my bag in my hurry to get out of the car, feeling furious and humiliated.

A small, stout man comes up to me.

"Actually, 50 rupees is a fair price," he tells me. "It's the 'Indian' price."

Now this really pisses me off.

"The man at the information booth told us that we should pay 20 rupees!" I state defiantly.

He shakes his head violently. "Ask him again," he demands. "Ask him again."

His furious response, added to the insanity of these runaway prices, breaks my confidence. Suddenly I'm no longer sure what the tourist officer said. I decide that he's right. I need the tourist officer to restore some sense of order to this chaos. If I can get him to restate the fair price, maybe it will give me the leverage I need to pay a reasonable fare.

The man follows me into the station.

"How much did you say a taxi to Dasaswamedh Ghats should cost?" I ask the man behind the counter.

He looks over my shoulder at the man behind me and his face grows pale.

"35 to 50 rupees," he says.

I'm stunned. What am I going to do now?

"What did he say," asks the man, gloating in triumph.

"35 rupees."

The man turns red with rage.

"I heard what he said," he tells me. "For you, now the price is 60 rupees."

He storms outside and yells, "60 rupees! 60 rupees!"

The crowd takes up the chant and the price has gone up again.

Tarun and I look at each other helplessly. Then, off in the distance, outside the parking lot, near the main street, I spot a lone taxi.

"There," I grab Tarun's arm and point. "Let's go. Quickly." We run towards the taxi, leaving the taunting drivers behind.

"Dasaswamedh Ghats," I tell the driver.

"35 rupees," he responds.

"The price should be 25 rupees," Tarun begins.

"Let's just pay him the 35 rupees," I interrupt.

"What do you mean? We know the fair price is 25 rupees."

"I don't care. I don't want to keep fighting these guys."

"Jason, he's ripping us off!" Tarun shouts.

I take a deep breath. During our stay at the Mahatma Gandhi Ashram I saw a quote on the wall of Gandhi's hut that still resonates in my mind. It read: "The essence of lying is in deception, not in words; a lie may be told by silence; by equivocation, by the accent on a syllable; by a glance of the eye, attaching a peculiar significance to a sentence; and all these kinds of lies are worse and baser by many degrees than a lie plainly worded." These words shook me to my core. I had always told myself that I was an honest person, but when I read this I realized it was not so. I have always been so afraid that people would not like me, that I never contradicted anyone. Whenever I disagreed, I simply kept quiet. I had thought that because I had not spoken a lie, it was not my fault if they believed my silence indicated agreement. Internally, however, I knew that this was not so. I knew that I had intentionally deceived them out of my fear of being judged or hurt. The quotation in Gandhi's hut made me confront my own cowardice. To keep silent because I am afraid to speak up is not honesty, and I have since resolved not to keep my thoughts or feelings to myself. Now I face a moment of truth. I have to tell Tarun what I think and feel, even though I know he will not agree and most likely will not respect my position.

"It's not worth it, Tarun. I'm tired of fighting over a couple of rupees. I'm happy to pay it if it lets us get out of here. You don't have to pay a thing. Okay? It's free for you. Let's just go."

His face turns red and his body quivers slightly. He opens his mouth to say something, closes it, and finally says, "fine."

We get in the car, and Tarun stonily turns his face towards the window. I know he hates being taken advantage of. It makes him feel helpless and weak, and he's not used to feeling this way. I also wish we didn't have to choose between fighting for a few cents and being swindled, but this is the reality here. Personally, I'm relieved to be headed towards our destination, happy to have avoided the humiliation of accepting the taxi drivers' vastly inflated prices, but my relief doesn't make it easy for me to sit next to a friend who's angry with me. It's the kind of response I knew I'd have to deal with if I want to be up front and honest, and now my job is to learn how to live with this and accept it so I'm not tempted to use deception or silence to protect myself from other people's disapproval. Hopefully this kind of bravery will help me find and face the truth about who I really am.

2.

From my taxicab window, I watch thousands upon thousands of people trudge through streets which are covered in dirt, mud, feces from emaciated and diseased cows, and red spittle from betel chewing old men. Our taxi driver, cursing continuously in guttural Bhojpuri, drives us down one narrow road after another. His first choice dead-ends in a massive pile of garbage. Dogs and beggars, picking at the remains, look up briefly as we turn around. We return to the main road, take another offshoot, twist and turn, only to dead-end again, this time by the river's edge. He spits red juice out his window and violently turns the wheel.

Even though I have the exact address of Mouna House, a hostel recommended by a friend back home, the driver can't find it. After thirty minutes of dead-ends and heated cursing, he resorts to asking people for directions. Most people sadly shake their heads in dismay, but after fifteen minutes we encounter a group of children who say they can show us the way.

They run in front of our car, laughing and jostling each other, until we reach a large, nondescript grey building lying in a small cul-de-sac. There are no signs on the house, but the number on the front is the same as the address I hold in my hand. I pay the driver, give the children a few rupees, and knock on the door. A moment later a window opens overhead and a disheveled, unshaven man sticks his head out.

He looks down at me and frowns.

"Is this Mouna House?" I ask.

"Yes. I am Mouna."

"Are there any rooms available?"

"Yes. One moment please."

The front door squeaks open to reveal Mouna, a portly Indian man wearing a t-shirt bearing a large dried coffee stain. His feet, bare and hairy, stick out from under his baggy blue pants. He scratches his belly absentmindedly. "Come this way," he says.

We follow him down a short, dimly lit hallway. He gestures towards an open doorway, and we walk inside. The available room is a rectangular box, empty except for the thick layer of dust on the floor. It has an attached balcony, overlooking tall trees, between which I catch a glimpse of the glimmering Ganges. A thick wire mesh covers the room's windows. "The wire mesh," Mouna tells us, "is to keep the monkeys out of your room. And be careful. Don't take food out on the balcony. The monkeys have been known to jump onto the balcony and snatch food out of people's hands.

"The room is 100 rupees per night. If you want to stay I'll get you two beds."

"Sounds great," I say. "We'll take it."

Mouna drags in two metal cots and gives us a key to the front door's padlock. "The door will be locked by ten. If you come in after that, please do so quietly. We have many students here and they need their sleep."

When Mouna leaves, Tarun addresses me. "Jason, do you really want to stay here?" He gestures dismissively at the rickety cots and the wire mesh on the windows.

"Yeah, why not. It's cheap, and I have a good feeling about Mouna."

"It's cheap," he says, putting his hands on his hips, "but I'm sure there are better hotels in the city."

A part of me wants to be agreeable. It's clear that Tarun wants to leave, and if I agree he'll be happy. But I want to stay. After facing taxi drivers and street vendors who relentlessly rip off tourists, I'm happy to be in a hotel run by someone who didn't try to beat us down and wrestle every last rupee from us. I don't want to have to wander around town with my bag on my back looking for something else. I hold onto my resolve to be forthright, and decide to tell Tarun what I feel.

"I'm sure there are nicer places, but at least we don't have to fight for a fair price, and I feel safe with Mouna. I don't think he's going to try to rip us off."

"Yeah, he seems all right," Tarun admits, "but I heard that there's great entertainment here. Let's go to a hotel with a bar, where we can meet some other people and have some fun."

Again, I feel the pull to give in and make him happy. I'm afraid that if I don't go along, he'll leave. I don't want to be alone in Varanasi. I'm not ready to tackle India without help. But I resolve to stick to Gandhi's exhortation: to try to act fearlessly and speak my mind.

"I don't want to drag my bag all over the city. I'm tired. Besides, I don't want to haggle anymore, and we can go to bars without changing hotels. I'm going to stay here where I feel safe."

Tarun pauses, and I can feel the icy touch of fear creep up my chest. Is he going to leave me after all? Will I break down and accede to his wishes?

"Fine." Tarun says finally. "I'll stay here for tonight, but I want to look around and see if we can find anything better. Okay?"

"Sure." I smile at him. "That's fair."

I'm relieved that he's willing to stay, and I'm proud of myself for standing my ground and speaking my mind.

We leave our bags in the room and set out to explore Varanasi. We want to visit the Ganges, but though we can see the river from our room, it's not obvious how to get there. We take a street that seems to be going in the right direction, but it twists and turns until I'm completely lost.

"Do you know where we're going?" I ask nervously.

"Don't worry," he pats me roughly on the shoulder. "I've got it under control."

"That's good," I reply. "I've got no sense of direction. I'd get lost here for sure."

Tarun smiles confidently, and I continue to follow him. The residential section we began in slowly turns more commercial, and shops and restaurants emerge between the homes. On the walls are menu selections of pizza, pasta, chow mien, omelets, cereal, and milkshakes, beckoning for tourists to enter.

The restaurants, shops, and people continue to grow in number, the indistinguishable mumble of people talking increases in volume, until we step out from a narrow alleyway and find ourselves in a major thoroughfare. Hundreds of people crowd this area. Vending stands sell pots and pans, fruit, statues, holy symbols, shirts, cameras, and shoes. Dozens of rickshaws sit by the side of the road. Emaciated cows stare at us with sadly human eyes. Small clusters of pilgrims, wearing dirty white robes and carrying wooden walking sticks, debate the mysteries of karma and rebirth.

"You did it." I say to Tarun.

"Of course. I told you I would."

A very large, broad set of stairs leads down to the Ganges. These are the ghats, special steps which provide access to water for bathing. Half naked sadhus wearing orange loincloths, touts, tourists, pilgrims, and even a few barbers sit on the stairs. My beard has grown quickly and after a month I'm very scruffy. The barbers look at me eagerly and hold up their blades. "Shave, sir?"

"No thanks," I smile down at them. "Maybe another time."

About halfway down the stairs we spot an elevated platform which overlooks the river. Tarun and I hurry over to it, eager to take in the view. A few young boys, holding large stacks of postcards in their hands, rush over to us. "Look, look! Good deal!" they shout.

"Not now," I duck away from the cards they thrust in my face. "Maybe later."

We push past the boys and walk to the edge of the platform. Bathing in the Ganges is said to wash away all sins. Could I wash away my troubles, cleanse my soul from its pain, and thereby find the secret to the happiness I long for?

I put my hands on the cool stone ledge and lean over. Below me, I see dozens of people crowded together in the river, directly in front of the descending steps. This tangled, shifting mass of humanity, interacts in such a confined space that I'm reminded of worms trapped in a container of moist dirt, crawling over and past each other in a desperate effort to find sustenance or freedom. Some of the bathers wash with a bar of soap, which leaves a small puddle of white spill around their bodies. Others simply scrub water onto their skin. Some people talk and laugh with their neighbors, while others close their eyes, pour handfuls of water over their heads, and then descend beneath the river, hands clasped in prayer. The various bathers conduct their business, public and private, in such close quarters it's hard for me to understand how they can keep track of what they're doing.

The spectacle of all this humanity, and the undistinguishable roar of voices, distracts my attention from the water, for a while at least. Eventually, however, I notice what's wrong with this picture. Pots, pans, sandals, food containers, and bits of colorful junk float on the surface of the river, which itself is so opaque and brown it has the appearance of a dark cup of coffee. And when I follow the trail of refuse down the river, I notice a group of government workers dredging garbage out of the water, collecting all manner of unidentifiable rubbish. I tap Tarun on the shoulder and point to them. He grimaces in disgust.

"What do you think?" I ask Tarun. "Do you want to go in?"

"I've always wanted to bathe in the Ganges."

"I'd love to go in too. But it looks pretty gross. I don't know if I can do it."

"Let's go down," he suggests. "Maybe it's not as bad as it seems."

It's not. It's worse. The river is so muddy I can't see even an inch into its depths. There's no telling if there are pots and pans, animal bodies, or even syringes beneath the undulating opaque surface. Reality overwhelms my desire for a transcendent experience. I'm afraid to have even a drop of this water touch me. I'm certainly not going to bathe in it.

"I can't do it, Tarun. You go ahead if you want."

"Shit!" He looks at me with teary eyes. "Let's see what a boat ride costs."

Tarun walks angrily towards one of the boat vendors. "How much?" he snarls.

"Thirty rupees each," he says.

Tarun looks at me and I nod my head. We actually have no idea what a "fair" price would be, but our perception of fairness is much more important than the actual amount of money we spend.

The vendor leads us to a long, wooden rowboat. The boards, which twist slightly with age, groan softly when we step aboard. A skinny Indian man sits in the middle of the boat, oars crossed in front of him. The vendor sits behind him and puts a metal bucket on his lap. He smiles at us.

"The boat is a little leaky," he confesses. "But don't worry. I'll bail out the water as we go."

We sit down, and the oarsman slowly maneuvers us away from the shore. As we pull away, our view broadens in scope. I can see that the crowd of bathers congregates directly in front of the Dasawamedh Ghat itself, and unused, uncongested water stretches out along the shore on both sides of them.

From a distance, the bathing looks different. Crowded as the water is, people perform intimate functions side by side, allowing each other enough space so that everyone can engage with the river in the manner that they wish to. It was chaotic, noisy, and unsanitary up close, but from here I get a sense of shared community – the entire spectrum of human life, people's different needs and desires, from the holy to the mundane, all accepted without judgment or hostility.

I've never seen anything like this in America, where we separate religious and secular actions, but here, despite, or perhaps because of the endless crowds, each person makes use of the Ganges in their own way. Washing clothes and gossiping co-exist with meditation and prayer. I'm warmed by the non-judgmental, accepting attitude the bathers have to embrace in order to use the river together.

We row slowly down the Ganges. Many boats traverse the river, some small and dingy like ours, others large and modern, but there is sufficient room and our boat slowly maneuvers itself into open space, giving us an unimpeded view of the coastline. Red, pink, yellow, and brown buildings line the shore, while ancient stone temples, situated directly on the river's banks, ripple quietly in the water's reflection. Handfuls of people bathe in front of some of the ghats, but most are empty. The twenty-minute boat ride is peaceful and serene, precious commodities in urban India.

Off in the distance, huge clouds of smoke and flames erupt into the sky. As we get closer, the crackle and hiss of the fire shatters the tranquility of the river.

"Those are the Harishchandra and Manikarnika Ghats, otherwise known as the burning ghats," our guide explains. "Those flames are never allowed to go out. We believe that anyone who is cremated there goes directly to Heaven. Please don't take any pictures. The priests don't allow it."

Our guide picks up his oars and places them on his lap. We float slowly past the burning ghats, watch the flames stretch towards the apex of the sky. It's a thundering, sobering statement about the ultimate finality of life, and I pause to reflect on my journey. I could decide that a month in India is enough. I could go home and talk about the adventures I've had, and feel good that I've done something that most people I know would never do. But, would I be happy with this?

Buddhism encourages its' disciples to contemplate their own deaths. The hope is that people will accept the transient nature of physical reality and use this knowledge to help them act according to their highest principles. Someday, I know, I will be on my own deathbed. At that time, if I were to look back on this trip and contemplate the choices I made, will I feel satisfied that I spent a month in India, even though I never found my true calling, or a path to personal happiness? I would not. I would wonder about what might have been, and I would curse myself for not being strong enough to stay until I understood why I was drawn here.

At the same time, the flame and hiss of the final fires reminds me that if I were to die in India tomorrow, I would be proud of myself for taking the risk and at least allowing for the possibility that my inner guide could lead me to happiness. I will never feel satisfied with my life if I know I settled for less than what might have been possible. I look at the fires and renew my vow that I will not return home until I have found the answers that I seek.

3.

Before going any further, Tarun needs to cash in his remaining Traveler's Checks. He's almost completely out of Rupees, and if he doesn't get a new infusion he won't even be able to pay our rent.

We enter one of the major banks, and I feel intimidated by the large, imposing building, the thick and sturdy doors, and the burly bank guards, who carry massive guns. I feel like I've entered a modern version of the Wild West, where the bank has to be prepared to defend itself from armed thieves. I keep my hands in my pockets and try to look non-threatening.

Though the bank is not air-conditioned, the lights are turned off and it's pretty cool inside. I sit on a chair along the wall, close my eyes, and try to rest while Tarun takes care of his business.

I hear people begin to argue. I listen to their voices rise in volume and temper, and I think smugly to myself that whatever is going on, I wouldn't be shouting like that. Not in this place. Not with those guards so close.

A tap on my shoulder brings me out of my reverie.

I turn to my right, and a bearded tourist nods his head towards the shouting. "You'd better go save your friend," he says.

I suddenly realize that the angry voices belong to Tarun and the small woman who was waiting on him.

"They're all like that!" Tarun shouts.

The woman, whose head barely can be seen above the counter, tries to sound tough.

"Sir. I can't accept these. There's no need to shout."

"You're being unreasonable!" he shouts again. "Just listen to me. I already signed them. You have to take them. Do you understand? You have to take them!"

"Sir. I already told you. I cannot take them. If you keep shouting at me, I'll have to get the manager."

"Good. Go get the manager. Maybe he'll have some sense."

The woman turns around and storms away.

I walk over and touch Tarun's shoulder.

"What's going on?"

He's so angry, he's panting.

"She won't accept my signature."

"Why not?"

"My signature isn't consistent. I never do it the same way twice. It's just the way I sign my name. If you look at the checks, you can see that all the signatures are different."

He hands me the checks, and I see that it's true. It looks like five different people signed his name to the different checks.

The manager, a short Indian man wearing a brown tie, steps up to the counter. The woman Tarun was yelling at stands triumphantly at his side.

"Sir. Are these yours?" The manager asks.

"Yes. Let me explain..."

The manager cuts Tarun off. "We cannot accept these. These signatures don't match."

"Yes. I know. But if you'll just look you'll see that they are all different. That's how my signature is."

"These signatures don't match," the manager says curtly. "We cannot accept them."

"But you're not listening. That's my signature. It never matches. If you look carefully you'll see..."

"No," the man says sternly. "I have looked. They don't match. We won't accept them."

"But you have to accept them!" Tarun screams in desperation. "I've already signed them. I can't use them anywhere else!"

"Yelling at me won't help you. We are not going to accept these. Not now. Not ever. Take them and go."

"Why are you being so unreasonable?" Tarun wails.

"Do you want me to call the police?" the manager asks.

"No…but you have to listen to me. You have to cash these checks. I already signed them."

"No, sir. You are wrong. *I* don't have to do anything. *You* have to leave. *Now*. One more word, and I'll call security."

By now the whole bank is watching. Tarun, stiffly immobile, can barely control his rage.

I decide to intervene. Maybe it's possible to salvage this situation.

"Sir," I ask politely.

The man looks at me.

"I'm sorry my friend got angry, but he needs the money, and he's already signed these checks. If your bank won't use them then he's lost his money."

"Your friend should have thought about that before he started shouting."

"I know. I'm sorry. But if you'd look at the checks closely, you'll see that they all have different signatures. He's not trying to cheat you. It's just that he always signs his name differently."

The man hesitates, and I have a brief moment where I think he may actually do us a favor. Then he shakes his head.

"No. We cannot accept these. You should get your friend out of here before he gets into trouble."

"Why are you being so unreasonable?" Tarun shouts again.

The manager loses his temper.

"You were abusing my employee! You are shouting at me! It is you who are being unreasonable. We have been very reasonable. Get out of here – *now* – or I will have you thrown out."

With that the manager and the woman turn and walk away.

"Wait!" Tarun shouts.

I put my hand on his shoulder. He looks down at me.

"Come on. Let's go." I say, gathering his signed traveler's checks.

"But Jason. We can't go."

"Come on. We'll cash these somewhere else."

"Where?"

I look over the counter. Both the manager and the woman have turned back around to watch us. I have a feeling the manager enjoyed standing up for his female employee. He might enjoy having the guards throw Tarun out of the bank, too. As a general principle I don't like messing with large men who carry big guns.

"We'll work it out. Let's just go."

Tarun allows me to guide him away from the counter. His anger is gone, and he's practically lifeless as I drag him out of the bank.

"Jason, that's all my money. If those checks are worthless, I'm broke. What can I do?"

Outside, we sit on a curb.

"Let's look in the guidebook and see where else we can go."

"But I can't use these checks anymore." Tarun's hangs his head morosely, his hands are clasped tightly between his knees. "I already signed them."

"We'll see," I say. "Let's find a travel agency. The rate won't be as good, but their standards might not be as high."

"What if no one will take them? I'll have to go home."

He's completely crestfallen, as if his trip is already over. I feel terrible. He's just a man in his early 20s, trying to find himself. Like me. I'm pretty sure that I have more money than I need. I won't let his trip end just because he can't cash his traveler's checks.

"If we have to, I'll lend you some money."

"Really? I don't know if I can accept that."

"Let's hope you don't have to. Come on. There's a travel agency nearby."

I marvel at my confidence. Suddenly I'm able to act like the fearless, compassionate man I'd like to be. I know it's easier to be fearless when the problems I'm facing are not my own, but I wish I could be this way all the time.

The travel agency is a little office within a shopping plaza, which has one desk and a small counter with a cash register. We sit at the desk and an Indian man, the only person working in the office, comes over. I take out and sign some of my traveler's checks, hoping to set a successful tone for our business. There's no problem with my signature, and he cashes my checks without difficulty. Once I've got my money, Tarun hands the man his signed traveler's checks. We hold our breath as the man looks them over. After a moment, he goes over to the cash register and counts out the correct exchange rate. When he gives Tarun the money, we're so relieved it's hard to keep from laughing. We thank him and get out of the office as quickly as possible.

Tarun is so happy he jumps up and down for joy.

"We did it, Jason!" He wraps me in a bear hug. "Thank you! I can finish my trip now! Thank you!"

"I didn't do anything." I can barely get enough air into my compressed lungs to speak. "But I'm glad you got your money."

"Come on!" Tarun says. "I'll buy you lunch!"

4.

For lunch I order pizza, which despite being nothing more than tomato sauce and melted cheese on toast, tastes great. Anything vaguely familiar is comforting at this point.

After lunch we decide to visit the Benares Hindu University, which has a famous temple called the New Kashi Vishwanath Temple. The majority of the well known temples only allow Hindu believers into their sanctuaries, but this particular temple is open to everyone, so I'll be able to enter. In addition, we've been told that the words of the Bhagavad-Gita are written on the walls in English, so perhaps I'll have a chance to learn some Hindu wisdom, and see if anything moves me, strikes me, or hopefully, helps lead me to the insights I'm looking for.

We approach a bicycle rickshaw wallah to see what he'll charge for our planned excursion. A bicycle rickshaw is essentially a two-seated bicycle, where the rear seat is a large canopied carriage seat and the front seat is a regular bicycle seat. The passengers sit on the rear seat, in the shade, while the rickshaw wallah, fully exposed to the elements, pedals. It's a typical Indian dilemma. I get to sit in a padded seat while some man exerts his effort lugging me around. It doesn't feel right, and it isn't right, but the fact is I have money and he doesn't. Although I am not comfortable with the way he earns his living, this is how he feeds his family. If I don't employ him, then his family may not eat. If I try to give him money without employing his services, I demean him. However, if we let him overcharge us, we feel like fools. Tarun and I decide that we'll salve our consciences by overpaying him. We'll try to fix a fair market price, and when the ride is over, we'll give him a large tip.

Despite our best efforts to be clear, our conversation becomes confused, partly due to the driver's poor English, but mostly due to the odd head bobbing motion he makes while talking.

In America, when we want to communicate with a head motion, we have only two options: the vertical "yes" nod and the horizontal "no" shake. Indians have a third option. It's a motion somewhere in between. Imagine that the hinge your neck rests on is loose. If someone bumped into you, your head might wobble back and forth slightly, tilting first towards one shoulder and then back towards the other, until it regained its center of balance. This is the Indian head bob.

Indians frequently do this while we're talking to them. Neither Tarun nor I understand what it means. It seems like they're agreeing with what we're saying, but when we finish speaking they may suddenly contradict us or argue. It's very confusing. Eventually, I'll learn that this motion means neither agreement nor disagreement, just, "I'm listening," but at this time we haven't figured it out.

After several minutes of intense haggling, our battle with the rickshaw wallah hits an impasse. We think the fair price should be about 160 rupees for the whole trip, but he wants 160 for each way. Although we actually plan to pay him the price he's asking for, we want it to be a large tip, rather than extortion. Finally, Tarun tries to demand that the driver accept our offer.

"We'll pay you 160 rupees. Okay. Let's go."

The man does his Indian head bob thing, and we get into the rickshaw, thinking we've reached agreement.

Despite the uncomfortable feeling which accompanies having a man pedal us across town, it's an interesting way to see the city. We're part of the busy life of the street, but as we're moving slower than it is, we have time to watch and absorb it. In addition, because we are in the rickshaw, street vendors can't harass us, so we can relax and simply take in the chaos, which finally allows me to observe Indian street life. It's like a living spider web – cars, motorcycles, rickshaws and pedestrians all weave in and out of each other's way, streams of life moving at different speeds and heading to or from the source of this city's life: the holy Ganges. From the shelter of the rickshaw, I can sense the order in the blare of noise and confusion. The way Indians naturally make room for each other, while strenuously pursuing their individual goals, strikes me as intuitively connected and vibrantly alive.

Eventually, we pedal down a quiet, tree lined street that leads to the temple – a squat orange stone building with a tall white spire erupting from its center. Our rickshaw driver parks his vehicle in the shade of a small tree, within easy view of the temple's entrance. He's not interested in visiting the temple, but we've hired him for the return trip as well, so he'll wait for us.

The noise of India immediately vanishes once we enter the white marble hallways. The temple is not only clean and elegant, but it's the most spacious and serene building I've been in in India. Statues of Hindu gods reside in several enclaves, illustrations adorn the many walls, but it's the ornate black script of the Bhagavad-Gita that truly captures my attention. It tells the story of Arjuna, a charioteer in the service of Lord Krishna who finds himself preparing to engage in battle with a great enemy host. All of the combatants are clansmen, and when Arjuna sees his relatives on the other side of the battlefield, he begins to have doubts. Is it right for him to fight his own kin? And when he sees the size and strength of the enemy, he despairs. Can we win this battle? He speaks of his doubts and fears to Krishna, who advises him on how to stay on the spiritual path, what different spiritual paths exist in Hinduism, and what it means to do your duty.

The question of duty, in particular, strikes me as important. I'm looking for a sense of purpose. I'm looking for happiness. But how do I know whether I'm doing the right thing? How can I know if I've done my duty, to myself, to my friends and family, or to the creator? Krishna offers several pieces of advice:

You have control over whether or not you do your duty, and how you do it, but you can't control the results of your work. The fruits of your work should not be your motivation (2.47).

Do your duty to the best of your ability…abandoning worry and attachment to the results of your work. Remain calm in both success and failure (2.48).

Work done with selfish motives is vastly inferior to work done selflessly…(2.49).

As the ignorant work, fully attached to the selfish fruits of their labor, so the wise should work without attachment, for the welfare of society. (3.25).

I feel a sense of peace waft over me as I read these verses, as if a burden has been lifted. This wisdom, the idea that we should examine the value of our labor without attachment to the results, strikes me deeply. As a writer, I understand that the best essay does not always win the contest. The best speech does not guarantee success in a debate. Even a great book may never get published. Does this mean that these authors have failed? And, if I spend six months in India, truthfully search for illumination, courageously face my fears, yet find that I still do not know all the answers about how I should live my life, will I have failed? According to this text, the answer is no. Success and failure are issues that, ultimately, are out of my control. What is within my control is the quality of my work, the effort I make, and the type of work that I do. I had already realized that my need to be perfect was harming me, but I did not know what else to strive for. I now understand that success should be evaluated on the basis of whether I did my best. This is what I can control. This is what I should strive for. Anytime I honestly do my best, I should be proud of myself, regardless of whether my work is perfect or what results it achieves. My job, while in India, is to do my best. I need to be open to following my intuition. I need to have the courage to go where it leads. If I do that, I will have done my job. I can't control whether I will find the wisdom I seek, but I can make sure I do not give up prematurely, and I can hold onto my faith, that the experiences I seek will come my way, as they have in the past.

Another aspect of the story that intrigues me, occurs when Krishna advises Arjuna to learn to control his mind. If he lets his fear or his doubts overwhelm him, he will not be able to do his duty. On the other hand, if he can learn to control his mind, he will be able to hold fast to his duty and to his truth. Krishna tells him that:

Anger gives rise to delusion, which creates confusion in the mind. When the mind is confused, reason is destroyed. One loses sight of the right path when reasoning is destroyed. (2.63).

A disciplined person, who experiences the sensual world with senses that are under control and free from attachments and aversions attains tranquility. The attainment of tranquility eliminates all sorrows. The mind of such a tranquil person soon becomes completely steady. (2.64 - 2.65).

There is neither Self-knowledge nor Self-perception to those whose senses and mind are out of control. There is no peace without Self-perception; and without peace there can be no happiness. (2.66).

A mind wherein all desires rise and dissipate without creating any disturbance, as river waters flow into the ocean without creating a disturbance, attains peace. One who craves material objects is never at peace. One who abandons all desires and becomes free from craving and the feeling of 'I' and 'my' attains peace. (2.70 - 2.71).

The mind can be one's friend as well as one's enemy. The mind is the friend of those who have mastered it, and the mind acts like an enemy for those who do not control it. (6.05 - 6.06)

Before I started meditating, I accepted the philosophic bromide I learned in school: I think, therefore I am. I believed that there was no difference between my "mind" and my "self." During the meditation course, however, I began to question this belief. If I am my mind, why was it so hard to meditate? I wanted to sit and focus on my breath, but my mind would float away and reminisce about the past or fantasize about the future. It was a struggle to get it to concentrate on what I wanted, which made me wonder: how was it possible for my mind to want something different from what I wanted? After all, if I was my mind, then how could there be a disagreement between what I was interested in and what my mind was interested in. On the other hand, if the mind could wander away from a subject that "I" wanted to consider, then the mind could not be me.

In fact, thinking distracted me from meditation. It took me out of the present moment and unbalanced my mind. Which made me wonder: Did ceaseless thinking get in the way of experiencing existence?

The more I meditated, the more I studied my mind, the more I believed out of control thinking did get in the way of being present to life. During meditation there were moments when I was able to suspend thinking for a few moments, when my concentration became so intense that thoughts fell away, and I felt more vibrantly aware and alive than I did at other times. In fact, I remembered how, when I was a child and I played little league, there would be times when I could focus on the ball without thinking about anything at all. Everything would be quiet, and only the ball would exist in my consciousness. Despite the fact that my mind stopped thinking, I felt like I existed more intensely and purely than at any other time.

I'm beginning to believe that the mind is simply a tool of consciousness, like my hands, which I can use to interact with the world. It helps me exert mastery in the world, but it's still a tool I need to learn how to monitor and manage. The Bhagavad-Gita describes this endeavor, and reminds me not to let my thoughts, my fears about what may or may not happen, my doubts about what I can achieve and control, or my concerns about what others may think, undermine my confidence. My previous travels taught me that I can follow my intuition, that it will lead me to experiences that can change my life for the better. I have to control my mind, resist its doubts and fears, while using it to help me navigate the decisions that lie before me. Doing this will help me hold onto my faith that I can and will be guided, that I will ultimately discover what kind of work will fulfill me.

It's late afternoon by the time we're ready to head back to the hostel. Both Tarun and I are ready to leave Varanasi, and we decide to have the rickshaw driver take us back to the train station to purchase our tickets. When we arrive, we hand him 160 rupees, thinking that we'll give him another 160 as a tip. He makes a negative nod of his head. "The price is 320 rupees," he says.

Tarun and I look at each other, surprised.

"We agreed on 160," Tarun says.

The driver shakes his head no. "320," he insists.

Tarun looks at him, infuriated. "You can't just change the price and expect us to pay!"

"The price is 320 rupees," he says stoically.

Tarun whirls towards me. "Let's just pay him the 160 we agreed on and be done with him," he says.

I look at Tarun. Then I look at our driver. Other drivers have tried to get us to go to restaurants and gift shops owned by their friends, but he pedaled us where we wanted to go without complaint. He never tried to take advantage of us, and he's not haggling with us now. He is simply stating what he believes to be the fair price. I don't know how it happened, but somehow we didn't communicate well when we negotiated this trip.

I turn back towards Tarun, hoping I can disarm his anger. "I know this sucks, but the guy pedaled us all over Varanasi. He deserves more than four bucks for that."

"You can't let him rip us off!" Tarun exclaims.

"What do you want to do? You know 160 rupees is not fair."

"But he's trying to bully us. He can't just demand extra money!"

"That's true. You're right. But what do you want to do? We just can't give him 160 rupees. That's not enough."

"It's all we agreed on."

"Yeah, I know. But there must have been a misunderstanding. Either way, it's not right."

"We can't let him rip us off."

I've had enough of this. How long are we going to fight over this when we feel he deserves the money anyway? "Forget it, Tarun. I'll pay him," I say, angrily dismissing his concerns with a wave of my hand.

"No, Jason. Don't do that." He puts his hand on my arm, stopping me from taking out my wallet. "Don't pay him."

"Tarun, if you don't want to pay the money, that's fine. I'd rather pay the whole thing and get this over with. We had a nice afternoon. Let's not ruin it by fighting over a few bucks."

Tarun watches me, helpless and fuming, as I take out my wallet and give the driver 320 rupees. The driver takes the money stoically and pedals away.

I turn back to Tarun, and he's staring at me. "Every time you allow yourself to be ripped off, it encourages them to take advantage of other foreigners."

"Come on." I take a deep breath. "We'd like to think we have some control over this, but we don't. The rickshaw wallahs are going to try to take advantage of foreigners regardless of what I do. Do you really think it would make a difference if we beat this guy down? Besides, that man pedaled us all over town. It would be wrong to pay him any less than we did."

"You have to learn to stand up for yourself against these people," Tarun insists.

"Maybe. But you also have to be realistic. How much aggravation is four dollars worth? You've got to know which battles are worth fighting."

We walk into the train station, each of us resisting the urge to continue an argument that can have no satisfactory ending.

"Look," Tarun says. "I'm going south to Tamil Nadu. That's where my family's relatives are. Would you like to come with me?"

I pause and consider. A frightened part of me is happy he made the offer. Despite our disagreements, I don't have to be on my own if don't I want to. But, as I search my feelings, I realize that I'm tired of feeling like I constantly have to compromise or fight for my point of view. At this point, I'd prefer to be on my own, so I can simply do what I think is right, without defending it. My mind reminds me of my early experiences, how helpless I was, how I got ripped off. And I'm afraid to be alone. On the other hand, my original idea was to be alone. In my previous travels, it was while alone that I found the inspiration and the experiences that helped me change. It's terrifying, but I know that it's time to face my fears and step out into the unknown.

"Thanks, Tarun. Thank you for the offer, but I think I want to visit my friend in Shimla."

The next morning, we wake early and head to the ghats to watch the orange and red rays of sunrise set fire to the Ganges. The sight of the glittering currents and the languid rowboats is truly beautiful, and it's fascinating to sit and observe the tranquility of the morning as it turns into the chaos and noise of the day. After breakfast, we pack our bags and say goodbye to Mouna. He wishes us luck, and we're on our way.

At the train station I say goodbye to Tarun.

"I hope you enjoy meeting your Indian family." We embrace, and I'm surprised to find I have to fight back tears.

"Thanks Jason. It was great traveling with you," Tarun says. "I hope you have a good time up north."

"Thank you. Good luck to you too."

I watch Tarun walk away, expecting to feel terrified, but I don't. Instead, I feel like a burden has been lifted from me and I want to laugh. My sense of joy has returned. I don't know what awaits me, but I suddenly know that the experiences I came to India for lie just ahead.

Shimla

The Varanasi train station is chaotic, crazy, and completely disorganized, which I now believe is what passes for normal. I wait patiently until I hear the loudspeaker's crackly voice announce my train. When it does I grab my bag and run up and down the train tracks trying vainly to determine which compartment is S2. Inevitably, the train begins to pull away before I've located my compartment, so I run to the nearest doorway, toss my duffle bag inside, and jump in behind it. From here I have to trudge through the train until I find my berth, which, while an unpleasant way to begin a journey, is not so bad when you know that this is as bad as it gets.

My compartment is overcrowded, as usual, but when I indicate that I have a berth here the three people sitting on the lower bunk move aside so I can join them. I'm surprised. Before, Tarun and I kept to ourselves and played cards on one of our beds until nighttime. We never sat with others, and it never even occurred to me that we could.

I squeeze in and smile to show that I'm friendly.

"I am Assam," one of the men says. "What is your good name?"

"Jason."

"This is Rajiv. To his left is Sanjay. And on the other end, that is Kunjar, Rao, Sena and Kanha."

"Nice to meet you," I say in my most chipper voice.

"Where are you from?"

"America."

"Oh. America. You know, I thought so. Tell me, may I ask you a question?"

"Sure."

"Good. We have television here, you know. Let me ask. Do all Americans really live in mansions?"

"No," I respond, laughing. "Like here, I think, there are both rich and poor. Maybe people in America are not as poor as people here, but not everyone is rich."

"I see," another man says. "What do you do in America?"

"Well, my last job was as an English teacher. I don't really have a career, though."

"And where do you live?"

"In New Jersey."

"New Jersey? Where is that?"

"It's close to New York."

"Ah! New York. Please, tell us what that is like?"

As we talk, people from neighboring compartments hear our conversation and move into our area. Some people sit on the floor, while others simply stand in the aisle and lean on the bunks or on the shoulders of a neighbor. As usual, I'm uncomfortable to be the center of so much attention. It's hard for me to imagine that anything I have to say is very interesting, but I guess it's not every day that they have a chance to question an American tourist. And despite the discomfort I feel, there is a part of me that relishes this situation. Maybe I've always wanted to be the center of attention, but was too timid to allow this to happen?

As we talk, one man, sitting on the opposite bunk, only a foot and a half away, puts his legs on my lap! No one seems surprised by this, and I assume that it must be normal Indian behavior. To test my theory, I pick up my feet and stretch them across the aisle, until they rest in the lap of the person diagonally opposite me. He doesn't even seem to notice. And, as our berth grows increasingly crowded, and as my neighbors get more and more excited, people thrust their faces within an inch or two of mine when they speak to me. So close, in fact, that it's hard to see their whole head as they're speaking.

It's hard not to feel claustrophobic, but I try to relax and accept the situation. Families sleep in the same room, share toilets with others or have to sleep and bathe outside. The concept of personal space as I know of it doesn't seem to exist here.

"New York is kinda like Mumbai," I say, "in that it is very crowded. There are so many people there and there are hundreds of cars on the roads. We also have many taxis there, like you have here, and it is very noisy.

There are hundreds of stores where you can buy almost anything that you want, and there are people on the street who sell watches, clothing, books, and almost anything you can think of. So, in those ways it is similar, but it is also very different. In New York, we have many different cultures. You meet people from all over the world. And we have restaurants and food of every kind; American, Chinese, Korean, Indian, South American, Italian, French, anything you can think of. And the buildings are so high, it's like they touch the clouds. You have to lean back as far as you can to see the tops of some of them."

"You have Indian food in New York?" one man asks.

"Yes. At home I used to love to eat Indian food."

"Is it like what you have eaten here?"

"No. Not exactly."

"What was different?"

"Well," I confide, embarrassed, "it's not as spicy at home. I can barely eat the food here."

They laugh, "too spicy!"

"You guys use too many chilies!" I complain.

They continue to laugh. "Americans like food so bland! Make it extra bland, please," one man teases.

"So," one of the men continues, "what are you doing in India?"

"I don't really know," I admit. "I heard that India is a spiritual place. I'm hoping something special happens. Right now, I'm going to Shimla where a friend of mine lives."

"Very nice," he says. "India is a very spiritual place. You have come to the right place. Surely, you will find what you are looking for."

People nod and smile, but we seem to have run out of conversation. After a few minutes of silence, one by one, people shake my hand, say goodbye, and return to their compartments to eat and relax. When it's over, I realize that not only did I enjoy the attention, but I answered all their questions honestly and no one seemed disappointed or judgmental. Maybe striking out on my own won't be so bad after all.

2.

I get off the train at a town called Kalka, and take a long bus ride through the mountains to Shimla. When we arrive, the bus driver lets me out in front of a small store. The man inside doesn't speak any English, but I mime using the phone and he allows me to call Dorje, the young man I'm here to see. He's a Tibetan monk of the Dalai Lama's order who I met briefly when he came to America to visit a friend of mine. At the time, Dorje casually remarked that I should come and visit him in India sometime. When he said it, I didn't take it very seriously as I had no intention of coming to India. Later, when that changed, I wondered if he really meant it. I didn't know what I would do if I visited him, but I wanted to know if it was a real possibility, just in case it seemed like a good idea once I got to India. Fortunately, he is a gracious human being. When I called him from America, he said that his offer was still valid, and when I called him from Varanasi the other day, he said that my timing was fine and he'd be happy to see me.

The phone rings and rings, and I'm afraid that he won't answer and I'll be stuck in this store for who knows how many hours, but, eventually, someone does pick up.

"Hello?"

"Dorje. Is that you?"

"Yes. Jason! Where are you?"

"I have no idea. The bus driver let me off by the side of a road. I didn't see any street signs."

"Where are you now?"

"I'm inside a store of some kind."

"Is there someone there I could talk to?"

"Yeah. Hold on."

I hold out the phone towards the store owner, and he picks it up. He talks to Dorje for a few moments, then hangs up. I stand inside for a while, and then decide I'll be better off standing outside by the road, where Dorje might see me.

I stare into car windows as the traffic passes by. I wonder how or if I'll be able to identify my host. We only met twice, about a year ago, and I really can't remember what he looks like. More likely, he'll have to find me, though I suppose the white guy standing alone by the side of the road won't be too hard to identify.

Up the road, I see the small figure of a man walking towards me. He slowly gets bigger, and when I can see his features I see that he's smiling. This much I remember about Dorje – he's always smiling – and this gives him away, even if he has ditched his monk's robes for a pair of blue jeans and a blue sports jacket. We meet each other and embrace.

"Hi Dorje. How are you?"

"Very good! How are you?"

"I'm relieved to see you. I wasn't sure you'd be able to find me."

"Of course I found you. Come on, let's get a taxi."

He holds out his hand, and a taxi pulls over. We get in and he gives the driver instructions.

"So, Dorje, what are you doing here?"

"Oh. I am running a genzokan. This is Tibetan for old age home. This is our first project of this kind, and they have asked me to oversee it for a while.

"And, what are your plans? What will you do here?" he asks me.

"I don't know, really. What is there to do?"

"Not much," he laughs. "It's very quiet. Sometimes too quiet, even for a monk like me, but I'm sure you'll find something. And don't worry. You can stay as long as you want."

"Thanks, Dorje. Thank you."

Outside, I watch as we travel through the heart of the city and head towards its' outskirts. Buildings become more scattered, people and cars are fewer, and the roads steepen. We climb higher and higher, until we reach a long, winding road that leads up a nearby mountain. This road is only wide enough for one car, so when we encounter a car traveling the other way, we have to back all the way down the road to let the descending car pass. Once it's by us, we climb up the road again, only to encounter another car making its descent. Again, we back down and re-ascend, only to encounter yet another car descending. As we go back and forth, other cars arrive behind us, hoping to ascend. After the third descent, our driver refuses to go back down, and we're stuck at an impasse. Four cars wish to ascend, three more want to descend, and no one is willing to give way. People park their cars, honk their horns, and yell at each other.

Our driver honks his horn futilely for a minute, then gets out of his car to point and yell. The other drivers do the same, and I begin to despair. There's no telling how long this will last.

"How far away are we?" I ask Dorje.

"The genzokan is still a fifteen or twenty minute drive away."

"And if we walk?"

"At least forty or fifty minutes. But it's steep. Your bag's pretty heavy. You don't want to walk so far with it."

We wait five minutes, but the drivers get no closer to a resolution.

"Come on," I open the car door. "Let's get out of here."

"Ok," Dorje shrugs his shoulders. "If you say so." He pays the driver, and we walk away from the traffic jam.

The uneven, rocky mountain edge flanks us on the left as we walk up the steep one lane dirt road. Isolated, lonely houses appear at random intervals. Here, a large home with a wrap around balcony and big windows. There, a small wooden shack, with warped wooden walls and a sagging roof. Then, a small white building, with two steps leading to an open door.

"This is our general store. I need to stop in for a minute," Dorje says.

Inside, Dorje speaks to a portly Indian man, wearing a smudged white smock. He nods his head, walks into a back room, and returns with several white envelopes.

"The postal service doesn't go to the top of the mountain," Dorje explains, "so we use this store as our mailing address. In return, we buy all our supplies here."

We leave the store and continue up the mountain. I don't see any people, animals, or birds. Only the sound of the wind breaks the silence. And the occasional sound of my grunting, as I move my heavy bag from one shoulder to the other.

Up ahead, there's a young man. He sits on a dirty, frayed, once white blanket on a small outcropping of stone next to the road. His face and hands are smudged with some kind of black substance. Dozens of pairs of shoes and sneakers surround him.

"What's he doing?" I ask Dorje.

"Oh, he makes a good living. Everyone comes to this man to get his shoes fixed. He's always busy."

Dorje shouts something in Hindi, and the young man laughs, looking shyly at me. I remember, suddenly, that Dorje likes to tease people.

We climb for another 45 minutes before we see a large, white, square structure jutting out from the side of the mountain.

"That white building is the genzokan." Dorje says. "Above it, to the left, you see that red building?"

"Yes."

"That's our monastery. And there, at the very top of the mountain, do you see the red and yellow building?"

"Yes. Barely. It's way up there."

"Yup. That's the Hindu temple. It has to be the highest building. Otherwise, people will get very angry. We don't want to offend anyone. We are happy where we are."

Twenty minutes later we arrive at the old age home. A pack of unkempt dogs bark at us as we pass through the small courtyard which marks the entrance of the building. At the end of the courtyard is an open doorway, where 40 men and women stand in line, waiting for us. They bow as we pass. Their wrinkled faces smile warmly. Many hold prayer beads in their hands. A few hold large prayer wheels, which they spin continuously, sending good wishes into the cosmos.

I bow and say, "Tashi Delek." It's the only Tibetan I know, but it's nice to be able to say hello.

"The residents wanted to come out and greet you," Dorje proudly informs me. "They perform all the services at the home. They buy the food, cook the meals, set up the dining hall, and clean the rooms and the dishes."

"What's left for you to do?" I tease him.

"Oh, I run the center. I have to get money to pay for everything. I have to take care of all the government paperwork. I have to pay taxes. I have to get permits for the building we want to do. I take people to the hospital when they are sick. I have to do everything. But you'll see. Maybe you can help me.

"On the top floor, we have the two VIP rooms. My room is the smaller one, but I get the TV. You will sleep in the other room. You should be honored. It has the genzokan's only private bathroom. You can stay here as long as you like. Make yourself at home."

"I'm in a VIP room," I ask, surprised.

"Yup. Is that okay with you?"

"Sure," I reply, thinking, happily, that coming to Shimla already seems to be working out.

3.

The magnificent expanse of night sky astonishes me. It stretches out across the heavens like a sparkling black sea. The stars are so bright, it almost hurts my eyes to look at them, and they are so close, I feel if I tried I could reach up and touch them. I stay outside and watch until the cold, slowly seeping into my bones, forces me to go to sleep.

Or, I should say, I try to go to sleep. My room, luxurious and large and private as it is, is made of concrete, without any rugs, carpeting, or insulation. The wind whistles through a gap between my window and the wall, bringing a constant, freezing cold draft into the room, stealing every trace of warmth I manage to exude into my half dozen blankets. And getting up at night to go to the bathroom, even though I don't have to leave my room to do it, is absolutely unbearable due to the constant draft and the ice-cold, concrete floor.

In the morning, I feel exhausted and stiff. I can't wait to have a hot shower, but when I turn the shower dial, nothing happens. Not even the sound of water trying to get through creaky pipes.

"My shower isn't working. Or, I can't figure it out," I tell Dorje, feeling dirty, cold, and irritable.

"None of the showers work," he replies nonchalantly. "I have the pipes for hot and cold running water, but I haven't been able to get the permits I need to get the water connected to us. In India, to get government officials to approve something, I have to bribe them. If I don't, somehow my paperwork always gets lost. But it's very tricky. If I give one man a bribe, his superior might find out and want something as well. There's a lot we haven't been able to afford yet. I'll get you a bucket of water. Wait here."

Dorje goes into the public bathrooms and emerges with a metal bucket filled to the brim with water.

"Take this into your shower. Do you have soap?"

"Yes."

"OK. Don't take too long. Breakfast will be ready soon."

I take the bucket into my cold, concrete shower, and strip out of my dirty clothes. The water is freezing cold, and having to pour this icy water over my body, while standing in the constant draft, is torture. It's November, it can't be more than 30 degrees, and I'm sincerely worried about getting frostbite. I scrub furiously, rinse, and dry off as quickly as I can, shivering so hard that my teeth knock together painfully. Afterwards, I decide that body odor is not really such a terrible thing. If I limit my physical activity, and try not to exert myself or sweat, maybe I won't have to bathe while I'm here. I decide to shower only if I start to smell, and then only if the smell is so bad that I can visibly see it affecting other people.

As I get dressed, still shivering, I wonder why I'm here. When I contemplated separating from Tarun, I remembered Dorje's offer to visit and felt an inner tinge of excitement. I recognized this irrational feeling as a nudge from my intuition, and decided to follow its guidance, but now that I'm here I have no idea what I'm going to do.

After a breakfast of warm cocoa and bread, I sit on my bed, open a book, and settle into the tranquility of the mountains and the old age home. Whispered conversation, short bursts of laughter, the occasional barking of the residence's pet dog, and the methodical bat, bat, bat of the women who spend hours pounding grain into a fine powder that they use for baking, echo softly throughout the building. These subdued daytime sounds carry a tone of happiness and peace into my room, reminding me that I'm not alone.

The contented atmosphere of this place contrasts sharply with the old age home my grandmother lives in in America. There, the home radiates the silence of abandonment. People sit, muttering anxiously to themselves, waiting for visitors who never seem to arrive. Here, people smile in the silence. They nod and bow to me as I pass them in the halls. They sit together in loose circles and look out over the mountains. They hold their prayer beads in their hands and silently recite their mantras. They visit those who are too sick to leave their rooms, and bring them comfort and food and companionship. They have formed a close-knit community, rather than a collection of discarded elderly people.

I witness this closeness on my first afternoon. Dorje offers to play cards with me to alleviate our boredom, and just when I'm about to win, we hear people shouting. We rush outside and see four old men struggling to carry something heavy up the stairs. As we run forward, I realize that they're carrying a woman's prone body. For a moment, it looks like a sure catastrophe. They're all going to fall down the stairs, and we'll be left to tend to their broken bones. But, miraculously, they make it up the stairs. As quickly as they can, they shuffle and carry the woman to one end of the corridor. Two women rush to meet them, holding a chair in their outstretched hands. The men gently put the old woman in the chair and turn it so she can look out over the valley. With the men panting around her, and the two women looking on anxiously, the old woman's face breaks into an enormous grin. Dorje and I look at each other in disbelief.

"They're crazy!" Dorje says, shaking his head.

"What was that about?" I ask.

"Ah," he scowls. "That woman is very sick. She has to stay in her room. It's too painful for her to do more than sit up, so people have to bring her her food and take care of her. Before she took ill, she used to always put a chair in that spot and watch the view. I guess some of them decided to let her see her beloved view again."

Dorje turns and walks away. I follow him. "They could have killed themselves," he says. "Then I'd have to take them to the hospital."

"Yeah," I respond. "I guess so. It looked pretty dangerous."

Dorje considers this, then turns to me, smiling. "I guess love can be dangerous. But it sure makes life worth living."

4.

In the evening, several monks come down from the monastery to meet me. They gather around Dorje and me, and with Dorje translating, they ask me where I'm from and what I'm doing here. Before I left for India, I completed a certification course in teaching English, and subsequently taught in a language school for six weeks. Dorje mentions this experience, and the monks ask him to convince me to teach them English. I'm hesitant to agree. My total experience is very slight, and though it had been a life changing experience for me, I'm not sure I can recapture its' magic.

Still, what do I have to lose? And what else am I going to do?

"Do you know if there's somewhere I could buy English textbooks?" I ask Dorje. "I guess I could try to teach a class, but I'll need some help."

"There are some bookstores in the mall. I'll have my assistant take you tomorrow."

"Then, tell them okay. But tell them that it will only be for one month."

He translates, and they shout and clap their hands.

"They're very happy," he says. "There is a classroom in the monastery that you can use. They get foreign visitors sometimes, so they would like to learn some English so they can speak with them. They want to know if you can teach from 9:00 to 11:00 in the morning?"

"Sure. That sounds perfect, but tell them the day after tomorrow. I want to get those textbooks before I start."

Dorje tells them, and they rush back to the monastery to tell everyone the good news.

The next day, Dorje introduces me to his assistant Thilay, a tall, fat
Tibetan man dressed in maroon monks robes. There's a look of mischievous
humor in his eyes as he shakes my hand, and he smiles so brightly that I
find myself smiling back.

He looks at Dorje and unsuccessfully tries to suppress a giggle as Dorje
gives him his instructions.

"I've told him to take you into town and help you find some English
language textbooks. I've told him not to waste time," Dorje says seriously.
"You're supposed to go to a bookshop and come right back."

Despite Dorje's stern warning, our short errand to buy English
books takes all day. Our first obstacle is the fact that Thilay walks with
a pronounced limp. His right foot juts away from his body at a seventy-
degree angle, and his right arm is likewise bent at a ninety-degree angle,
clasped tightly to the side of his body. Later, Dorje will explain that Thilay,
like most of the monks in Shimla, is an escapee from Tibet, who risked
his life trekking through the Himalayas in the hopes of finding religious
freedom in India. He traveled at night, survived on cold rations, and hid in
the snow during the daytime. Because it was too dangerous to light fires,
which might attract Chinese soldiers, many of the monks suffered severe
frostbite and now have permanent injuries from their journey. Even worse
than the limp, however, is the fact that whatever caused Thilay's physical
damage also impaired his memory. This is a tragedy for a Tibetan monk. In
their tradition, the first thing an aspiring monk must do is to memorize all
the Tibetan holy texts. This generally takes from three to five years and no
progress or training can occur until the monk completes this task. Due to
Thilay's poor memory, he will never advance beyond the status of novice
monk. As a kindness, the monks permit him to sweep the temple and
polish the temple's statutes, but he is not allowed to live in the monastery
with the other monks. Instead, he lives at the genzokan and his main duty
is to assist Dorje.

Despite this depressing and probably embarrassing reality, and despite
the fact that Thilay knows that Dorje insisted our journey should be quick,

he still can't help himself. He must talk to everyone he sees. As he speaks, he becomes so animated and his laugh is so infectious, that I often find myself laughing, even when I have no idea what he's saying. It's simply a joy to be around him.

We visit several bookstores, but I find very little of use. There are no English textbooks and no grammar workbooks. The only useful items I find are a children's picture book of the alphabet and an English/Hindi dictionary. When I agreed to teach in the monastery, I assumed that I'd be able to find a book to guide me. Having to create a series of lesson plans, from scratch, was not my intent.

I consider backing out of my agreement, but what do I really have to lose? The worst-case scenario is that I try to teach them, they don't learn anything, we all get very frustrated, and in a month they'll be eager to send me on my way. And I remind myself of the passage of the Bhagavad-Gita which spoke of doing one's best, without worrying about the end result. I'll simply do my best and see what unfolds.

Besides, it was a desire to be open to life's mysteries, and my human connection to them, that led me to come to India in the first place. I believe that if I am open to it, life will lead me. I imagine that I can be led to teach the class in the same manner that I believe I'll be led to experiences that will help me change my life. I'll go to the monastery each morning, and try to be open to being guided. I'll listen to my inner voice, with the hope that each day it will become clear to me how I can use my skills to teach my students whatever it is that they need to learn. And, I acknowledge to myself, this better work, because I have no idea what the Dalai Lama's disciples need to be able to say in English, and even if I did know, I really don't know if I'd be able to teach it to them.

5.

The next morning Thilay escorts me to the monastery. The moment I enter, a monk grabs a chair and rushes it over to me so I can sit down, while other monks bring me a cup of butter tea and a piece of bread. It feels odd to have a group of the Dalai Lama's monks, reputed to be some of the holiest people in the world, serving me and hovering around me like I am the honored guest.

I'm not thirsty or hungry as I just had breakfast, but I politely accept the items and take a sip of the tea. I try not to visibly gag. It's so creamy, it has the texture of melted butter, and so rich I feel sort of nauseous. With the help of the bread I manage to force it down.

"More tea?" one of the monks asks me in accented English.

"No thank you," I say quickly. The last thing I want is more tea! "Classroom. Teach." I point to myself and at the monastery. They nod their heads and lead me into a large room, filled with chairs lined in four neat rows. On one wall are two blackboards and a few pieces of chalk. The opposite side of the room has two large windows, made out of an opaque, milky white material that allows the room to fill with light, but prevents us from looking outside at the scenery.

I don't know how they know, but once I'm in front of the room, two dozen maroon robed monks silently file in. They sit quietly at their desks and look at me patiently.

I look out at them, and wonder what I'm going to do. I remember that Dorje said they would like to be able to communicate with visitors. To do that, they'll need to learn how to introduce themselves. I guess that's an appropriate place to begin.

I walk up to the chalkboard and write, "I, you, he, she, they, we," in a vertical row. I put one finger on the written "I" and point to myself and say, "I," out loud. Then, I walk up to the nearest monk, take his hand, point his finger at his chest, and say, "I." I look at him and repeat this until he says it with me. "I." "Good," I say, and walk to the next monk, where I repeat this procedure. Once each monk has done this, I go back to the board and write, "I am Jason." Then, pointing to myself, I repeat this. "I am Jason." As I say it, I run the finger of my free hand under the words on the board. Then, I take the hand of the first monk and point his finger at his chest.

"I am Jason," he says.

"No," I say, shaking my head no. "I am Jason," I say, emphasizing the 'I' and pointing to myself.

"I am Tenzin," he says uncertainly.

"Good," I say, smiling. I move on to the next monk and try again.

"I am Tsurtim," he says.

"Very good!" I reply. Soon, they all get it and they're nodding to each other and chatting in excited voices. I move onto the next concept. I write, "I am Jason. Who are you?" on the board.

I walk up to one of the monks, point my finger at myself, and say, "I am Jason." Then I point my finger at him. "Who are you?" He looks confused, so I do it again. "I" I say, pointing at myself, "am Jason." "You?" I ask, pointing at him.

"I am Gungbo?" he says, with a question mark in his voice.

"Yes!" I say, reassuring him. "I am Jason. Who are you?"

"I am Gungbo," he says with more authority.

"Good," I say, and I shake his hand. Then, I walk to the next monk. "I am Jason. Who are you?" When he responds, I shake his hands and move on to the next monk, until I've introduced myself to each of them. Once I finish, I get them to introduce themselves to each other. It's wonderful.

They are excited to be speaking English with each other, and they mill about laughing and shouting and shaking hands.

Now that they're learning and they're excited, I decide to push my luck. I ask them to sit down again by raising my voice, saying "Please sit down," and gesturing to the chairs.

When they are seated, I write, "I am Jason. You are Tsurtim. He is Gungbo." Then, I stand in front of Tsurtim and say, "I am Jason. You," I say pointing at him, "are Tsurtim. He," I say pointing at Gungbo, "is Gungbo." Then I try, "I am Jason. You are Tsurtim. He," I say pointing at Tsering, "is Tsering." I'm not sure how to explain the difference between you and him, other than through demonstration. I repeat this exercise a few more times, standing in front of different monks and changing who I point at for, "I am…You are…He is…" When I think they are beginning to understand, I go back to the board and write, "I am Jason. Who are you?"

I look at Tsurtim and say, "I am Jason. Who are you?" As he looks at me, I hold my hand under "I am Tsurtim," which is still written on the board. When I ask the question again, he responds, "I am Tsurtim." I laugh and run up to him and shake his hand. "Nice to meet you." I say.

"Who is he?" I ask, pointing at Gungbo. He looks at me perplexed.

"I am Tsurtim?" he asks.

"Oh." I say, running up to Gungbo. "Hello Tsurtim!" The class laughs.

"No," Tsurtim says, "Gungbo."

"Oh." I say. "Who are you?" I ask, pointing at him.

He hesitates for a moment, then says, "I am Tsurtim."

"Good," I say. "Who is he?" I ask, pointing at Gungbo.

"Gungbo." he says.

"Good." I run back to the board. I write, "He is Gungbo," and say, "He is Gungbo." This time, when I ask Tsurtim who the person sitting next to him is, he says, "He is Gungbo." "Great!" I say. After I try this a few more times with the class, they understand. Again, I have them stand up and ask each other questions. "Who are you? Who is he?" They run around the room, giddy with the joy of being able to communicate in simple English, and I watch them with pride. It's been a good first class.

The next day they again usher me into a chair and thrust tea and bread into my hands. As I feel myself forced to drink more of this gross tea, I realize it would be great if they knew how to offer food and drink. Then, I could refuse. Suddenly, I have today's lesson.

I take my ready-made props, the tea and bread, into the classroom, put them on the table, and write, "Would you like some tea?" on the board. I pick up my cup of tea and walk up to Gungbo. "Would you like some tea?" I ask him, holding out my cup to him.

"No." he says.

I sniffle, look sad, then pretend to cry. I wipe my eyes and walk to the next monk. "Would you like some tea?" I ask, holding out the cup to him.

"Yes," he says, probably hoping I won't cry again.

"Ah, good. Here," I say, giving him the tea. Then I write on the board, "Would you like some bread?" And I repeat the exercise. In a moment, they understand the question, "Would you like..." so I add the full sentence responses. "Yes, I would like some tea. Yes, I would like some bread." When I'm sure they understand, I stand them up and get them to offer each other tea, bread, an apple, a piece of chalk, a pencil, and some paper. Once they understand this, the lesson naturally leads into, "I am hungry. I am thirsty. I am not hungry," etc., to, "Is he hungry? Would he like some tea?" Etc.

It's at this point that I realize how beneficial it was to learn the pronouns first and to introduce the method of writing the pronouns on the board and conjugating verbs with them. I write, "I am thirsty, he is thirsty, they are thirsty, would you like, would he like, would they like..." Although I didn't plan it this way, I now have an actual teaching method to introduce new verbs and concepts. This excites me and further validates my trust that I can be guided by my intuition to create lesson plans that would help them.

As I watch them mill about, exchanging apples and tea, I want to pinch myself. I'm teaching monks how to express themselves in English! These young men spend their time learning, praying, and meditating – trying to turn their lives into moments of blessing for themselves, for others, and for everything that lives. It's breathtaking to think that I'm now somehow a part of the work that they do, and it's amusing for me to imagine that they spend part of the day learning from the writings of the Buddha, and part of the day learning from me. In fact, the milky white light, which illuminates the room, lends the entire scene a sense of mysticism, as if we exist in a room cut off from the rest of reality – a world where only study, companionship and laughter exist.

Which is the other aspect of this class that amazes me. When someone makes a mistake, everyone laughs, including the person who made the mistake, but I never see anyone look shamed by their mistakes. I never see anyone make fun of anyone else. They aren't competing with each other. They just laugh, help each other, listen closely to what I say and try their best. An ideal learning environment would, indeed, be free from shame and competition, but in America I wonder if this could ever happen. Here, they create this kind of atmosphere naturally.

By the end of the first week we have covered introductions, where are you from, do you have any brothers or sisters, would you like something to eat or drink, and comparisons, such as, is it hotter there than here? The monks can now greet and perhaps even get to know their guests. I almost can't believe it.

I arrived in India not knowing where I would end up, and I find, ironically, that I have been asked to become a teacher – and not just a teacher, but a teacher to disciples of the Dalai Lama. But what truly excites me, is the fact that I trusted that if I had faith, I could be guided to teach them what they needed to know. I had no lesson plan. I had no books to guide me. But simply by coming to class each morning and being open, the day's lesson came to me. Each lesson naturally followed the last, and by the end of the week the class progressed far better than it would have if I had tried to pre-plan the week.

I came to India knowing I would need to be guided, and the success of this class seems to demonstrate that if I can let go of my fear and embrace the day-to-day, moment-to-moment, reality of my life, I'll eventually be guided to my next experience. It's exciting to wonder what will happen next.

6.

My life forms a simple, pleasant routine. Every morning I wake at 6:00. At this hour it's still pitch dark outside, and the stars pulsate brightly overhead. I wrap myself in a heavy brown blanket and shuffle quickly to a small temple in the genzokan so I can meditate for an hour. I try to admire the sky as I hurry along, but it's cold and I never manage to do more than glance up as I pass by. I meditate for an hour, lock up the temple, and read in my room until 8:00, when Dorje wakes up.

At 8:00 I hang out in Dorje's room until one of the residents brings us breakfast, usually a pot of sweet tea (which tastes like hot chocolate) and cold, round, doughy pieces of bread. I don't imagine that this is a healthy breakfast, but it is filling and I enjoy it. Once a week we're brought a special breakfast of scrambled eggs, which, in contrast to the usual bland Tibetan fare, is especially tasty.

Sometime during our meal, Thilay will walk into the room. He'll smile and giggle, roll his eyes and throw his good arm about as he talks. Though I rarely know what he's talking about, I'll inevitably laugh with him. His presence is so full of joy, I can't help myself.

He hasn't learned as much as the other monks, but he has learned the concepts of "good" and "no good." He loves to tease Dorje with his new English. "Dorje. Noooo good," he'll say, emphasizing the word no, dragging it out so the oooo sound lingers. All I have to do is ask, "Is Dorje good?" to set him off in a fit of laughter. Dorje doesn't know how to respond to this. He smiles a tight smile and warns us that he'll get us back.

Thilay also uses his English to try to mother me. "More tea," he'll say, if I look cold. Or, "Food. Good. Eat." I refuse to acknowledge his entreaties unless he uses a full sentence, so he does eventually learn how to say, "Would you like more tea?" It doesn't stop me from saying no, but at least it gets him to practice some of the grammar.

After breakfast, Thilay and I walk up the path to the monastery, and I teach my class.

At 11:00 we return to the genzokan for lunch, which is usually a noodle soup called Thukpu, which, thankfully, tastes better than it sounds. The meal always comes with more of the gooey bread.

In the afternoon, we sit in Dorje's room and watch television. While American television can be credited with a multitude of horrible, tasteless, and pointless programs, I've never seen anything quite as bad as Indian TV. They've invented a genre I think of as the "karate musical": an incredible blend of awful overacting, poorly choreographed fight scenes, and sappy musical interludes, which include dozens of scantily clad dancers who gyrate around two inevitably estranged lovers who also happen to have mastered the art of the roundhouse kick. As we watch, I prod Dorje to explain the drama. He generally refuses under the guise that it's undignified for a monk to talk about such affairs as cheating on one's spouse, revenge, and the improbability of a poor orphan being a virtuoso violinist, who also is an expert at karate, who, surprisingly, is actually the son of a very rich politician, who was assassinated earlier, apparently without heirs. Oh, and the poor orphan secretly loves a fashion model, who is being wooed by an evil gang leader, but who secretly wishes there were some hero to save her and also provide her with a life of luxury. Fortunately, the actors overact so vigorously, and the plots are so flimsy, I don't need to understand the Hindi to follow the story.

When there are no movies on TV, we play cards. This is another image that always amuses me. I sit on the floor with Dorje, clothed in his maroon monk's robe, next to two young men who used to be monks, playing poker or gin rummy. We play solely for bragging rights, as gambling is a sin and

Dorje wouldn't participate for money. This is a good thing, because I never win. Even though we don't play for money, Dorje is very secretive about our games. He draws the red fabric "blinds" over the windows, which dims the light into a pink glow, all the while trying to make sure that none of the female residents take notice.

"You can't tell anyone about this," Dorje warns me the first time we decide to play.

"Why not? You said you don't play for money."

"That's true. But even so, many Tibetan people think playing cards is sinful. You probably noticed that there's always a game going on outside in the courtyard," he continues, noticing my confused look. "Some of the men play, just for a few rupees. Some of the women have come to me to demand that I stop them. Honestly, there isn't much to do here, so I don't mind that they do it, but I at least have to appear impartial. If the women ever see that I play too, it will be a big problem. And don't get any ideas. If you tell them, I'll tell them it was your American idea."

When we're burned out on TV and cards, we go to "the mall." Shimla was the summer home of the British government when Britain ruled India. At that time, Indians weren't allowed to walk the streets of the mall. Now, however, it is a thriving Indian marketplace where locals sell food and clothing. Spending part of the day here becomes my favorite activity.

From the monastery, we must descend the mountain path and travel to the outskirts of town where we reach a crossroads which leads to more populated city centers. It takes about 40 minutes to get there, but once there we can choose between taking a bus, riding a bicycle, or walking. If I go with Thilay, we'll usually walk. If Dorje is with us, he hates Thilay's slow pace and will urge us to take the bus.

But best of all, I love to rent a bicycle. A seedy, small man owns dozens of bicycles, which he rents for a few rupees for the day. They're dented, rusted – all of them obviously abused in some way – so we have to test them before taking them onto the road. The breaks, of course, are of paramount importance, but if the brakes work, then the seat is probably broken, which makes for a passable, but uncomfortable ride. If the breaks and seat are fine, then the handlebar bell may not work. To me, this is the most tragic scenario of all. It's the little handlebar bells that really make these rides fun.

Indian roads are often too narrow to accommodate more than one lane of traffic. Consequently, one of the unwritten rules of Indian travel is that smaller cars will pull off to allow larger vehicles to pass. In the case of the Shimla mall, however, vehicular traffic, with the exception of the local bus and police vehicles, is prohibited, which means that bicycles generally rule the road. I love to ride down the winding street as fast as possible, bear down on a large group of people walking in the middle of the road, ring my little bell, and cruise on through as they separate like the Reed Sea. I don't even have to slow down. Somehow this never ceases to give me a feeling of supernatural power.

When I'm not thrill-seeking, or rotting away watching terrible television, I help Dorje raise money to pay for the home's expenses. To do this, he's relying on the generosity of foreigners, mostly Europeans, who support Tibetan causes. He hopes to get some of these benefactors to "adopt" a resident of the old age home. Every afternoon, Dorje brings one or two of the residents into his office and asks them to tell me their history. They sit in a chair, humbly bow their heads, and slowly tell the story of their lives, which Dorje translates into English for me. I type it up on an ancient manual typewriter, and Dorje puts it in a promotional book he is creating to allow potential investors to read the residents' stories and choose who they might want to help support.

Even before I knew their backgrounds, I marveled at the difference between this old age home, and the one my grandmother lives in. My grandmother's home is a beautiful, spacious building – well lit, with a large cafeteria, a nurse's station on every floor, a movie theater, and even a room full of pets to play with. Yet, despite all the magnificent accommodations, it's a depressing place. Old men and women sit alone in plush chairs and stare absently into space. Each person waits forlornly for a visitor who never seems to come. In general, they seem to have been cast off by their families who must be too busy to deal with the burden of elderly relatives.

Dorje's genzokan, on the other hand, provides an example of what an old age community could be like. Residents spend time with each other, help each other, and help run the center if they are able. The sound of laughter and conversation echoes throughout the grounds. People never look at me with longing, anxiety, or fear. They smile, seem relaxed and even happy to be here.

And when I interview them, it's even more remarkable. They're almost all alone. Their families either live far away or have passed away. They never wait for visitors because there's no one to wait for. They know that their lives are going to be lived here, and I think it helps them that they aren't living their lives through younger people.

But what really strikes me is how happy they are in light of the hardships they endured. Most of the residents fled Tibet when China invaded in 1959, and most of them ended up in India. The Indian government provided them with asylum, but not freedom. They were not granted citizenship, nor were they given work visas. If they wanted to stay, they had to do the work that the government assigned them. At that time, the government was having trouble finding people to build roads in the Himalayas, where it was freezing cold, and in the South of India, where workers faced the oppressive desert heat. In addition to the severe temperatures, Indian road building methods were primitive. It was backbreaking labor, and poisonous tar fumes filled the air. Workers earned enough to buy one skimpy meal a day – usually a cup of tea, a piece of bread, and perhaps a few vegetables.

For decades, many Tibetan families lived like this. Inevitably, mothers, fathers, sisters, brothers, sons and daughters, perished while forging roads in India's most extreme climates. Those who survived worked until their bodies failed them. Then, no longer able to work, they were dismissed from their jobs. They had saved nothing. They had no skills and they had lost their families. Some found employment selling knickknacks by the side of the road. Others rooted through garbage and slept on the streets.

After hearing one tragic story after the next, I develop a theory as to why they are so happy here. Residents purchase, prepare, and cook all the food. Residents clean the rooms and wash the dishes. Residents plan celebrations and help those who cannot help themselves. Unlike my grandmother, who has nothing to do, has no responsibilities, and unless a visitor arrives, has no reason to get out of bed at all, these residents are responsible for each other and for the center itself. Being needed, I believe, gives their lives meaning.

In addition, they are grateful for what they have. After years of loneliness and living on the streets, they have a roof over their heads, three meals a day, and companions. After years of being neglected and abused, they are cared for. After years of isolation, they now have a community in which they belong. They don't take these things for granted. They appreciate the simple joys of life, and, I think, this allows them to feel happy.

7.

While my Tibetan friends bask in simplicity, I dream of washing machines. When I put on my last pair of clean underwear, I have to face reality. The monks wash their robes on the concrete outside the monastery. I realize I have to do the same, or people will begin to smell me before I actually arrive.

I knock on Dorje's door, and he lets me in.

"Do you have a bar of laundry soap?"

"What do you want it for?"

"I want to wash my clothes."

"Give them to me," he says. "I'll ask one of the women here to do it."

"Why? I can do it." I'm not really sure I can do it, but I want to try. Besides, it's been three weeks and my clothes are filthy. I don't want anyone to see them like this.

"You can't do it," Dorje insists. "You'll ruin your clothes. Give them to me. The women will be happy to do it. They'll feel it's an honor."

Insisting that I can't do it is the perfect way to insure that I'll die trying. At the very least, I want to try before I give up. I mean, come on, I have a Masters degree. How hard can this be?

"Dorje, I'm not going to let someone else wash my dirty laundry. Do you have the soap or not?"

"Jason, don't be foolish. Give me the clothes that need to be washed."

"I can't do that. It wouldn't be right. Where can I find the soap?"

"Stop being stubborn. Bring the clothes here."

"I'm not being stubborn. All I want to do is wash my clothes. Are you going to tell me where the soap is, or not?"

Dorje sighs in a deep and exaggerated way and rummages through one of his drawers, finally shoving a bar of soap into my hands. "You're going to destroy your clothes. And it will be your fault. Don't come running to me all naked expecting to wear some of mine."

"Now that you mention it, I'd look good in one of your robes."

"Forget it. Robes are for monks. Running around naked is for monkeys. You really should give me your clothes."

"Thanks for the soap."

I leave the genzokan and lug my duffel bag up the mountain. I hope I'll be able to wash my clothes in peace, but it's not to be. Several monks are sitting by the concrete floor where clothes are washed. They watch me curiously as I fill up a bucket with water, and when I start soaking my laundry, they walk up to me and reach out for my clothes.

"No thanks," I say. "I got it."

As I set down to work, somehow word spreads that the new teacher is about to ruin his wardrobe. Monks rush out of the monastery, each trying politely to take my laundry from me, until the courtyard is filled with concerned monks, standing over me like worried old women, watching with horror.

"Please, teacher," Tsering, one of the more advanced English speakers says, "let us do that for you."

"That's okay, Tsering. I want to do it. Please, tell everyone to go back to what they were doing."

He says something in Tibetan to the others, but no one leaves.

This is becoming a nightmare. The worst part isn't their insistence on helping me, or their view of me as helpless, but the fact that if they don't go away they will see how incredibly filthy my clothes are. But there's no way to hide my embarrassment now. I dump my clothes in the bucket of water, put in the bar of soap and swish it around, hoping the water will lather up and the suds will hide the condition of my clothing. When I finally lay my clothes on the concrete and begin to scrub them, the monks become very agitated.

Gungbo, another advanced student, actually tries to grab my clothes from me. "Please, teacher. Let us do it. We want to."

"Thank you, Gungbo. Thank you for the offer, but I want to do it."

"No. Please. Let us."

"Thank you, but no." I know that they are trying to help me, and from the looks on their faces, I'm sure I'm doing something wrong, but at this point I can't stop. I refuse to give up before I've even tried.

Surrounded by concerned monks, I scrub my clothes, gently, into the wet, soapy concrete. Nothing rips or tears, and I hang them up to dry feeling like I've proven some kind of point. When they dry, however, I learn the smelly truth. My clothes are still dirty. Apparently, I don't know how to wash my clothes without a washing machine, but after stubbornly refusing help, I'm too embarrassed to ask what I did wrong. I decide that I'll wake up early tomorrow and try again. Maybe, somehow, the pressure of being watched inhibited my natural washing abilities.

But a strange thing happens. My dirty clothes disappear from my room, only to mysteriously return later, folded and cleaned. Apparently, they decided that if I won't listen to reason they don't have to be reasonable.

I walk into Dorje's room. I try to raise enough anger in me to at least pretend outrage, but I can't even manage that. Instead, I find I'm smiling.

"Dorje," I say, "someone took my dirty laundry and cleaned it."

"Oh, really," he says, not even looking up at me. "I wonder how that happened."

"Uh huh. I bet."

"Is it really so bad?" he asks me.

And I have to admit, "no, I guess not."

"So, stop whining. Believe it or not, I asked one of the female residents and she was happy to do it. Like I said, she felt it was an honor."

"Okay, Dorje. Thank you."

"You're welcome. No one wants to see a naked American anyway."

I leave his room, mulling over the idea that it made someone happy to have done this kindness for me.

8.

I see them everywhere, and every time I see one I stop and stare. People who live here consider them to be thieves, but not me.

I've heard that scores of monkeys live in a sacred grove, on the top of a nearby mountain, where there's a temple dedicated to Hanuman, the Hindu monkey god. I want to see them.

"No way am I going to hike a mountain just to see some monkeys," Dorje says. "And you'll never find it alone, so forget about it."

But I can't forget about it. I want to see the monkeys!

It's getting towards the end of November, and every day it gets a little colder. I decide that if I'm going to go I had better go soon, before it's too cold to climb the mountain. If I can't get company then I'll settle for someone to point me in the right direction. Since Thilay goes into town every day, I beg him to show me the path. "Monkey temple. Road. Show me. Please."

"Monkeys, no good," he says.

"I like monkeys," I tell him.

"Noooo. Monkeys no good," he says, shaking his head for emphasis.

"Come on," I plead. "Show me."

He tries to deter me. "Monkeys no good," he says seriously. I just laugh. Everything he says makes me laugh. I can't help it.

"Come on. Just show me. Show me path."

Thilay is too nice to refuse me anything, and he reluctantly leads me to the path. It's down a narrow road, overgrown with weeds and trees. When it starts to ascend the mountain, Thilay stops. "Climb, very…" he holds his hand at an upward angle, showing me what he wants to say.

"Steep," I say.

"Yes," he says, nodding his head. "Climb very steep."

"That's okay. I don't mind."

"No. You no go." Although I have trouble taking him seriously, I realize he's not joking around. He really doesn't want me to go.

"It's okay Thilay," I pat him on the shoulder. "You go home. I'll see you later."

He shakes his head.

"Thilay," I say, pointing back the way we came. "Go home. Go Genzokan."

He shakes his head again. "You no go."

Now I'm starting to get upset. I appreciate his concern, but I want to see the temple. He doesn't have to come with me. I walk on, hoping he'll return home, but he follows me.

We walk very slowly, due to Thilay's bad leg. Eventually we reach a place where a small path separates from the road and snakes sharply up the mountain. It's rocky and looks like a very difficult climb.

"We go. Genzokan," Thilay says.

"Yes, Thilay. You go Genzokan. It's okay. I'm safe. You go now."

He shakes his head no. I'm worried about him, and I wish he would return home, but I don't want him to dictate what I do. I continue to climb, and he follows me.

I don't know why he's being so stubborn. What's he protecting me from? We slowly make our way up the path by climbing on tree roots and large stones. It's very steep. Every few feet I have to wait for Thilay to catch up. In addition to his bad arm and leg, he's overweight, and he's wearing a bulky monk's robe. When we reach a place where the path levels off, he's panting and out of breath. It's clearly too late for either of us to turn back. We stop talking and keep on walking.

At a clearing, we find ourselves at the base of a hidden settlement. Small huts made of white wood emerge above us, while a group of Indian men and women stand in a field of something that looks like green wheat. They almost drop their machetes when they see us. The sight of a white foreigner and a Tibetan monk suddenly appearing in their midst must look very strange.

We walk through and pick up the path on the other side. At this point I'm glad Thilay came with me, as I would never have found this part without him. I realize that this is probably why he refused to let me go alone. It would be easy to get lost.

The path rises precipitously. Almost directly above us, through a thick canopy of trees, I see a white and yellow building. I hope it's the temple.

A rigorous twenty-minute climb takes us to our destination. I had expected to see an isolated, abandoned sanctuary, perhaps overgrown with vines, empty but for scores of monkeys climbing the walls or gazing at intruders from hidden, protected recesses. Instead, twenty Asian tourists stand in the courtyard in front of the temple, taking pictures and drinking tea. Off to the side sits a little peanut stand, as well as a little teashop.

No one seems to have noticed that we came up through the forest, and somehow Thilay and Dorje seem to have been ignorant of the large paved road which runs up the other side of the mountain.

I treat Thilay to a cup of tea and some crackers for making the journey with me, and we watch dozens of adult and baby monkeys scamper around and on top of the temple. The monkeys I have seen around town have been wary of people, but these monkeys are fearless. They climb on the tables and scamper under our legs without the slightest hesitation. They must know that no one is going to harm them in the vicinity of the temple of the monkey god.

The strange thing is that although the monkeys feel free to climb the walls and roof of the temple, they don't go inside, even though the doorway is wide open. While Thilay drinks his tea, I investigate. The adventures of Hanuman – a small brown monkey with a gold crown on his head, who swings on trees and cavorts around the jungle – are painted on the temple walls. There are no English plaques or explanations, so I have no idea what he's doing, but the pictures are vivid and large and bigger animals and creatures often look crossly at him, so I get the impression that the monkey god gets himself into a lot of trouble.

I go back out and we sit and relax. Thilay enjoys his tea and I observe the scampering monkeys. Suddenly, the sunlight vanishes. When we look up, fierce, dark clouds dominate the sky. We get up quickly, hoping to descend before the rain starts, but the moment we begin to walk down the trail a deluge bursts upon us. The trail becomes a muddy, rocky waterfall. We slide down a few feet at a time, catching ourselves on rocks or trees. A stiff wind begins to blow, and the rain turns to hail. I am dressed in shorts and a tee shirt, which are now muddy, cold, and wet. I envy Thilay's thick robes, but his mangled arm and leg make the descent much more difficult and dangerous for him.

We help each other as best as we can, and somehow manage to reach the bottom without breaking anything. We're both shivering and freezing cold. Thilay insists on stopping at every store we pass so he can buy a cup of hot tea. To me this only serves to extend and increase the misery of our trip as each time we step inside and warm up, we have to return outside and face the cold anew. I'd prefer to go straight back home, but I defer to Thilay.

Because, he might have saved my life. At this moment, if he hadn't come with me, I might be lost in the forest somewhere, soaked to the bone, shivering and scared, surrounded by screeching monkeys. My Indian friend sacrificed his own pleasure and comfort, not to mention his safety, to help me do something that made no sense to him. He did so because he realized that I was going to do it, and because he knew I would need his help.

Perhaps this is why he's always laughing. He knows the joy of giving, of self-sacrifice, and his generous, open nature, draws him into close, fulfilling, relationships. He led me to the monkey temple because he understood that I wanted him to. And I do feel closer to him because of his actions.

But how is this different from what I do? I often feel driven to put the needs of others before my own, and I've spent much of this trip trying to unlearn this, trying to learn to prioritize my own desires and beliefs.

So, what about Thilay's needs? Can he truly be as happy as he appears to be if he's always self-sacrificing? I guess he appreciates my taking the time to teach him English, and I know he enjoys my companionship as well. So, he gives and receives. What I've been missing, I think, is balance. My needs should not always come first, because then I'd be too selfish to have a true, caring, reciprocal relationship. But, I can't always put everyone else first, because then I secretly feel bitter and unhappy. There must be a middle way. A balance between giving and receiving. If I can find this, then I think I'll really have made progress towards feeling fulfilled and happy. Then I'll know I'm on the right path.

9.

One morning a rising swell of voices disturbs our breakfast. Dorje and I run out of his room, where we see the residents standing on line by the front door, holding long white scarves, called Katas, which are given to respected people, dignitaries, and holy lamas.

Two monks slowly make their way past the line of people. The residents bow deeply to the larger monk, who bends forward so they can wrap the Katas around his neck. Dorje leans over to me and whispers, "That's Tenzin." He's a tall, broad shouldered man, with close-cropped black hair. He appears to be in his thirties, and he accepts the offered gifts with a regal, proud incline of his head. I have heard about Tenzin. This is the monk whose vision brought this genzokan into fruition. Because of his hard work, forty lonely, elderly, Tibetans now have a place to live.

Tenzin emotes a sense of strength, power, and dignity. He slowly makes his way through the cordon of well wishers, taking the time to speak to each person before he moves forward. It's several minutes before he's free. He slowly climbs the stairs and halts in front of Dorje. Dorje embraces his friend and turns to me.

"Tenzin, this is my friend Jason. Jason, this is Tenzin."

"It's a pleasure to meet you," I tell him. "I've heard a lot about you."

"I hope at least some of it was good," he jokes.

"It was all good," I tell him seriously. He has used his influence to help people in need, and I'm a bit in awe of him myself.

"Tenzin is here to film a documentary about the home," Dorje interjects.

"Yes," Tenzin agrees. "I want to make something to show the donors. I want them to see what their money has built. Hopefully, they will continue to support this cause."

"And this is Jimmy," Dorje says, introducing the other monk. "He's a cameraman. He's going to shoot the video. Will you show Jimmy around?" Dorje asks me suddenly. "He needs to find a good place to shoot the genzokan. Why don't you try the Hindu temple? That has a great view."

I suspect that this is Dorje's way of having some time alone with Tenzin, but that's fine with me. Jimmy and I walk around the surrounding hillsides, admiring the beauty of the countryside and looking for a good shot. Jimmy takes his camera with us, and often asks me to look through the lens and give my opinion. Tibetans are polite and respectful people so I shouldn't take it personally, but I'm flattered to be asked just the same.

Eventually we make it to the top of the mountain where the Hindu temple dominates the skyline. From here we can see a panoramic view in all directions, and Jimmy spends a few minutes filming the genzokan from this distance.

That evening, Jimmy, Tenzin, Dorje, Thilay, and I eat dinner together in Dorje's room. As a senior monk in the Dalai Lama's order, Tenzin travels the world giving lectures about the Tibetan religion and campaigning against Chinese occupation of Tibet. He is used to being the center of attention, and he takes it for granted that we've assembled here to listen to him. For my benefit, he tells the story of how this project began.

"I often had to come to Shimla on temple business," he says. "One day, I noticed an old Tibetan man searching through a pile of garbage. I couldn't believe it.

"In our culture we believe that old age is for relaxation, meditation, and prayer. Hard work and suffering should be borne only by the young. When I saw this man, I felt horrible. I knew something had to be done. In our tradition, monks spend most of their time separate from society, praying and meditating in our temples. During holy days, we perform rituals for lay people, but we never had the idea of monks providing social services. One of the benefits of the Chinese invasion was that we emerged from our mountain seclusion and began to interact with the outside world. We had an opportunity to witness other religious models. The example of Mother Theresa inspired many of us. She used her influence to help others, and some monks began to understand that we could do the same. This home is the first, the beginning of a new role that monks have to play in Tibetan society."

"This home is wonderful, Tenzin," I interject. "I really admire what you've done here. I've never seen a happier, more grateful group of people. If you don't mind my asking, you said you travel the world for Tibetan causes. What else have you been doing?"

"Have you heard about Thupten Ngodup?" he asks me.

"No. Who's he?"

"A few months ago," Tenzin answers, "we had a very high profile demonstration in front of the United Nations. We wanted the world to remember how the Chinese treat our people, but we were getting very little coverage by the media. Then, a man named Thupten Ngodup decided to do something about it. He lit himself on fire. Suddenly, every major world paper had his picture on the front page, and everyone was talking about the Chinese occupation of Tibet. He was a great martyr for our cause, and I am very proud of him."

This shocks me. "I don't understand," I say, interrupting Tenzin. "Buddhism preaches non-violence. Doesn't martyrdom go against this principle?"

Tenzin's face turns red. "We have to do something," he says, turning on me. "Our country is being destroyed. Our people killed. Our land polluted. Our religion suppressed. The whole world knows, but no one does anything. Do you think America will help us? Or Europe? No! Everyone is afraid of China. Everyone is greedy to trade with China. The world is turning away from us. But when that man burned himself, the world took notice. It was in all the papers. His sacrifice helped our cause. You know," his voice drops down to a whisper, "the Tibetan people are becoming frustrated. Non-violence and peaceful protests have failed. There are some Tibetans who are planning violence. Maybe they'll hijack a Chinese plane. Maybe they'll kill some Chinese soldiers. Maybe then the world will notice us again."

I'm stunned. In light of his anger, I know it would be wise to keep quiet. I'm not Tibetan. I don't have relatives in Tibet who suffer at the hands of the Chinese. I haven't been thrown out of my homeland and forced to live in lands that are strange to me. But it's disillusioning to hear a Tibetan monk advocate violence. And, I remember the words I read in Gandhi's hut. To keep silent would be akin to pretending that I endorse the monk's words. If I don't want to lie to him, I have to express my opinion.

"Tenzin. I don't understand," I begin hesitantly. "One of the things that I admire most about the Dalai Lama is that he has never advocated violence. Despite the harm and pain he has felt at the hands of the Chinese, he has never spoken against them, but always manages to reach out to them and call them his brothers. This is something I admire about him and about Buddhism in general. As a Buddhist monk, you can't advocate violence, can you?"

"What do you know about it?" he shouts, glaring at me. "Soon it will be too late. The Chinese government is flooding the Tibetan plateau with Han Chinese. Right now, they almost equal the number of Tibetans living in Tibet. Soon they will outnumber us and we will be a minority in our own country. An oddity for tourists to look at and not a people any longer! Soon it will be too late. What has non-violence achieved? We must act now!"

He stops to catch his breath and looks at me closely. "What about you?" he says suddenly. "What religion are you?"

"Jewish," I reply hesitantly. Part of me is always on guard for the possibility that people I meet will be anti-Semitic.

"Ah. Jewish." He sits back in his chair, pauses for a minute. "Maybe you can understand. For thousands of years, your people had no homeland. You know what it's like to live among strangers. You know what it's like to long for your ancestral home. Now, you have it again. If an Arab country invaded Israel, enslaved your people, forbade the practice of your religion and tortured your religious leaders, wouldn't you want to fight back? Would you be content to sit and do nothing while the world ignored the plight of your people?"

His words chill me. Newspapers often hold accounts of people who fervently hope to see Jerusalem's streets run red with Jewish blood. For an instant, I imagine the scene. I imagine the horror of watching my people destroyed, defeated, and repressed. I can easily imagine the world ignoring it or implicitly condoning it. And I feel alone. Helpless. Angry. It makes me want to throw up.

"Of course I would want to fight back," I concede. "It would be horrible. But would that mean that it's okay to kill?" I can't get past the idea that a Tibetan monk would advocate violence. He's supposed to believe in peace and love! "And even if you do fight back, what good would it do?" I continue. "You can't defeat the Chinese army. Can you? Besides, that's what I admire about the Dalai Lama. He rises above bitterness and revenge. And as a people, the Tibetans have been that example too."

"And what has it gotten us?" he asks. "It's almost too late."

I should stop. I can see that my words have hurt him, but I want him to be like the Dalai Lama. I want him to show me that people can hold onto their ideals, even in the face of violence. Even when they feel despair. "Do you really think you can force the Chinese to leave through violence?" I insist.

He thinks about that for a long moment, and his shoulders sag. "No. Maybe it is hopeless. But it is hard to do nothing."

Tenzin, usually so powerful and sure, is suddenly subdued. His right hand rests loosely on the table, forming a limp fist.

Jimmy, Dorje and Thilay sit quietly, looking down at their food. No one expected this confrontation. No one expected me to openly criticize their hero.

I take a bite of my now soggy meal. This is not the encounter I anticipated. This is not the conversation I hoped to have with my new friends.

Outside, faintly, I hear a monkey howl. I wonder if it feels as confused and frightened as I do. What should I have done? Should I have pretended that suicide by self-immolation didn't horrify me? I couldn't do that and still feel I was being honest. But, by judging Tenzin, I have shamed a good man. How was that a good idea?

We finish our meal in muted silence, mumble our goodbyes, and walk to our respective rooms. After I close my door, I stare out the widow into the infinite blackness, and wonder what will happen now.

10.

The next day, I slip out to meditate, but instead of going to Dorje's room for breakfast, I stay in my room. Is Dorje angry at me? Has Tenzin asked him why he allowed a disrespectful American to live in the old age home he built? I'm afraid to find out, and I hide in my room and read.

Eventually, I hear a knock on the door.

"Come in," I say hesitantly.

Dorje sticks his head inside.

"Is everything all right?"

"Fine, thanks. I'm just reading."

"Oh. Do you want to get some breakfast? It's ready?"

"Sure."

I follow Dorje into his room. A pot of tea and plate of the round, doughy bread awaits us.

We sit down and begin to eat. I'm afraid to say anything. Is he angry? Is he upset? Did I embarrass him?

Dorje takes a sip of tea and catches my eye. "Jason, would you be willing to interview Tenzin for his film?" he says in a nonchalant voice.

"Of course. I'd be honored," I reply. "What would I have to do?"

"Don't worry about it. He'll tell you everything."

"Okay. I'll do my best."

"Great. I'll tell him after breakfast."

I watch Dorje carefully. Does this mean that they're not angry with me? It occurs to me that Tenzin's coming to the temple at this time might not be a coincidence. How often do they have fluent English speakers here? But I'm grateful that they have asked me to do this. It's a way to show them I appreciate their kindness, and perhaps, a way to make sure there are no hard feelings after last night.

A few hours later, Jimmy knocks on my door. "Are you ready?" he asks.

"Sure. What do I have to do?"

"We're going to shoot the interview outside the front entrance," he says. "Follow me."

We walk outside, where Tenzin energetically paces back and forth. "I thought we should shoot the video here," he says. "This way donors will see the building in the background. It will remind them that we have made good use of their money."

We set up a couple of chairs in front of the doorway, I'm given a large black microphone to hold, and Tenzin and I sit down. Jimmy focuses the camera on us, and Tenzin gives me my instructions.

"First, introduce yourself and me. Tell them my name, that I am a senior monk in the Dalai Lama's order and that it was my idea to build the home that they see behind us. Then, I'd like you to ask me how I got the idea to build this home. Then, ask me if this is a common practice. I'll tell you that it is a new idea for us. Monks used to be rather secluded, but we got the idea from Mother Theresa that we could help in social causes as well. Then, ask me how many residents we currently have in the home. How many we would like to have. What we still need to accomplish and how I hope that this can be done. Okay?"

My head is reeling. "Wait," I say. "Can we practice this?" But before I can even complete my protest Jimmy shouts, "Action!"

I quickly try to gain my composure. I look at the camera, hold the microphone in front of me, and say, "Hello. My name is Jason Kurtz, and I'm sitting beside Tenzin, a senior monk from the Dalai Lama's order. Behind us you can see a genzokan, which is Tibetan for old age home. It was Tenzin's idea to build this home, and I'm here today to ask him about what led him to embark on this project. Mr. Tenzin, could you please tell us about how you first got the idea to build this home?"

"Yes," Tenzin says, launching into the story of how meeting a homeless Tibetan man changed his life. As he speaks, I hold the heavy mike out to him, listen to him and make "um hmm" noises to show that I'm engaged, all the while desperately trying to recall what he wanted me to ask him next. But Tenzin is so absorbed in telling his story and hitting all his points that he's forgotten that this is supposed to be an interview and not a lecture. I'm left frozen in place, holding the increasingly heavy microphone out in front of me, desperately praying that I won't drop it. He talks for a full fifteen minutes and I manage to make conversation noises until he finishes and Jimmy mercifully yells, "Cut!"

I put down the mike and massage my arm while Jimmy and Tenzin discuss something in Tibetan. I'm pissed off. I didn't enjoy sitting in front of the camera like a piece of statuary. Granted, this is about raising money for the old age home and not about my ego, but I was excited to participate. I want to complain – I can do better than that! Give me a chance. – but I stifle my resentment. This is Tenzin's show, not mine. And I don't want to challenge his expertise or methods again.

Tenzin walks back to me and sits down. "Can we do it again?" he asks me awkwardly. "I got a bit carried away and forgot to wait for you to ask me the questions. This time I'll wait and let you interview me." It's not much of an apology, but I don't need much. I'm excited again. "No problem," I tell him, realizing that the false start will actually be helpful. Now that I've heard his speech, I should be able to remember what points to cover.

We reposition ourselves and Jimmy yells, "Action!" This time Tenzin allows me to conduct the interview. He waits for me to ask him questions and I lead him through the whole story from his original idea, the raising of funds, the compatibility of Buddhism and social action, and the goals and concerns of the future. When we complete this take, we're all happy. Everything went smoothly, and we covered everything. Tenzin and I shake hands and Jimmy packs up his camera.

I feel good about the job I did, and I'm happy that I have been able to repay some of the kindness they have shown me. But what really amazes me is that Tenzin showed no trace of rancor from our argument last night. I'm generally afraid to argue openly with others because I worry that they won't like me if I do. Now, the cynical part of my brain argues that Tenzin didn't allow himself to hold a grudge because he needed my services. But, I wonder if that's true. What if he simply doesn't mind that I had a different point of view? What if he respected me enough to allow me my own opinion?

A week ago, I had an opportunity to witness some of the Tibetan students debate each other as part of their winter exams. The two monks faced each other, while their classmates encircled them. One man spoke, slapping his hands and stomping his foot each time he made a point, while the other listened, waiting for his turn to respond. As the points were made, the other monks smiled and laughed and nodded their heads along with what the young man was saying. Throughout the contest, I never saw anyone, even the opponent, look angry or upset. Just as I experienced in my class, everyone appeared to have a good time. I didn't see desperation, or the fear of losing, in either monk, nor did I feel the onlookers were judging the contest in this way. They appeared to be more communal than combative, more supportive than competitive.

So, perhaps Tenzin didn't feel he had to convince me, and perhaps he didn't feel ashamed that I disagreed with him. What if, even if my words upset him, he respected my right to have a different opinion? What if, while I waited for him to attack me back, he didn't feel attacked at all? Is it possible to cultivate a relationship where each person respects the other's right to their own point of view, where each person can disagree even about important matters and still care for each other? I can only imagine how free I would feel if I could believe my relationships were strong enough to survive intense disagreements. Maybe then I wouldn't spend so much time being afraid. Certainly, I think, it would help me have the courage to truly be myself.

11.

"It's the most horrible place in India," Dorje says gravely. "You would be wise to stay here instead."

It's the last week in November, and I've decided to leave. While I enjoyed my time in Shimla, and though I love teaching my English class, I've been searching for a sign as to what I should do next. One of the fantasies I had, when I was in America dreaming of coming to India, was that I would visit Calcutta and volunteer with the Mother Theresa Mission. Over the past few weeks, whenever I thought of going to Calcutta for the month of December, I felt the sense of joy that I've come to understand as the gentle prodding of my intuition. The feeling has gotten stronger as the end of November has neared, and I believe that it's time for me to go. Dorje, Thilay, and my class, all ask me to stay in Shimla, but something's pulling me and I'm determined to go.

For my last class, I decide to teach them a song, for fun. One of Dorje's poker buddies told me he learned "You are my sunshine" as a child, and now it's the only English song I can recall. Explaining what it means to be "my sunshine" is, admittedly, difficult, as I don't know how to say analogy in Tibetan. But it doesn't matter.

For the first time ever, I don't worry about singing off-key. The students are so free from judgment, and so full of love, that I'm sure my squeaky voice won't upset them. I write the words on the board, and sing the song. As I do so, the students sit up in their seats and murmur excitedly to each other. For a moment, I'm confused. Then, it dawns on me. My voice isn't cracking. I'm not off key! And I sound pretty good. Maybe, I could always sing. Maybe I just needed to relax and let myself do it.

After my second solo rendition, the monks join in. Three rows of five students each, straining eagerly, hands folded on their maroon robes, belting out the verses of a strange, yet happy song. Their voices are like broken chalk scratching the black board, and the words are foreign, but they simply plow through their mistakes. And, as they have in every previous lesson, they laugh at their mishaps, tease each other, and allow the confusion to become part of the comedy. By the end, we're all holding our sides, laughing and having fun.

I do, however, have to control my urge to cry when I hear them sing "please don't take my sunshine away." I certainly don't think I'm their "only sunshine," but I have brought them some happiness. And they made me feel worthwhile too. I'll miss my maroon-robed, off key, class.

After the class, I return to the genzokan to retrieve my things.

"You are welcome to return, anytime," Dorje says.

"Thank you, Dorje. I can't begin to thank you."

"Then come back," he says again. "As soon as you realize that Calcutta is a shit hole, come back. We'll be here."

Calcutta

I'm lost. My guidebook has a map with the Mother Theresa Mission located on it, but I can't find it. Fortunately, a group of children spots my confusion and races over. "Mother Theresa!" they shout in chorus.

"Yes!" I reply, stuck between relief and suspicion.

One of the children takes me by the hand as they escort me down a dark, narrow alleyway to a giant blue doorway. I ring the bell and wait until it opens. A small Indian woman wearing the blue and white robes of a Sister of Charity waves me inside. I can feel the children shrinking back into the shadows, avoiding the woman's presence, and I wonder what this signifies. Are the children in awe, or is it possible that even the Sisters of Charity don't want homeless children begging for food and money outside their door?

I step in and find myself inside a large, dimly lit, light blue hallway.

She watches me patiently and waits for me to speak.

"Is this the Mother Theresa Mission?" I ask, feeling like a fool for starting the conversation by stating the obvious.

She nods her head yes.

"I'd like to volunteer."

"Come back at 3:00. The Volunteer Coordinator will be here then."

I thank her and she ushers me outside and closes the door behind me. Somehow, without saying so, she made it clear that I was only welcome inside the Mission within strictly defined time schedules and boundaries.

The children surround me as soon as I'm back in the light of the street. They thrust a little girl to the front. By the unfocused look on her face I can see that she's mentally disabled. In addition, her right leg is twisted and lame. She limps forward and grabs my hand. Suddenly she and the other children are pulling me along the street.

"Sir," one of the children says. "She needs special milk. Will you buy it for her?"

They utter their request as they push me into a store, where the man behind the counter has, without being asked, put a very large box of powdered milk on the counter. When I shake my head no he replaces it with a smaller one. I take my hand out of the girl's grasp and leave the store.

The children run after me. "Please sir," they cry, "buy me some candy?"

I remember how Niranjan played with the street children of Nasik, before giving them money to share with each other. When they left him, they were laughing and happy, and it was clear he had performed an act of generosity and charity, and had not been taken advantage of. Ever since, I've wanted to follow his example. I pick up the little boy in front of me, thrust him high in the air, and place him down next to me. He laughs happily, but before I can take a step, another child is in my way. I push her gently out of the way, and she laughs as well. But other children block my path. I continue to play this game of picking them up, but our fun evaporates as their laughter is slowly replaced by begging. When it becomes clear that they won't let me go away without giving them a donation, I kneel down in front of the boy who appears to be the leader and give him a few rupees.

"Now share this with everyone," I tell him, proud to be following Niranjan's example.

He grabs the money and runs off. The other children don't follow after him as they're supposed to but instead thrust their hands out to me and beg.

"Go on," I say. "He has to share."

"He won't!" they plead. And I think they're right because the boy is already out of sight.

I try again. This time I give some rupees to one of the girls.

"You have to share this with everyone," I say in what I mean to be a stern voice.

She turns around and runs off, leaving the other children with their hands out, their faces stuck somewhere between hope and despair.

I try once more. When this child also runs away without sharing his money, I give in. Each child gets a few rupees, courtesy of the naïve American. It seems that Niranjan's magic is not so easily acquired.

2.

Back in America, when I visited my family doctor to get inoculated for this trip, he offered to give me the number of another patient of his, who was about my age and had been to India a few years before. Although I am a shy person and rarely go out of my way to meet strangers, I decided to call. I didn't know why, but I felt that sense of inexplicable excitement that indicated my intuition liked the idea. I called him and we agreed to meet the following week.

I learned that he was a devout Catholic who had traveled to India specifically to volunteer at the Mother Theresa Mission in Calcutta. His eyes sparkled, and he actually seemed to glow as he described how meaningful his contact with the Indians was, how important it was for him to see that he could be giving, generous, and courageous in the face of need and pain. His enthusiasm inspired me. Working with the destitute and dying had changed his life – perhaps it could change mine as well. Before our meeting, it never would have occurred to me to visit the mission, but after talking to him I was convinced I had to go.

So, I return that afternoon. I inform the sister who opens the large blue door that I want to volunteer, and she takes me inside. Without speaking, she leads me to Matthew, a six foot four inches tall, skinny, pale, white volunteer coordinator, who, in his friendly and obviously well meaning demeanor, reminds me of my friend back home.

"There are six places where the sisters allow volunteers to help," he tells me. "Two homes for the destitute and dying, Kalighat and Prem Dam. An Orphanage. A home for mentally disabled men. A home for abused women. And a school. In order to volunteer at the school, you need to be able to commit to stay for at least three months. These kids have enough instability in their lives, and the sisters want to minimize this on our end. The home for disabled men is unavailable at this time, as a group of brothers from Canada are here and they have that covered for now. The home for abused women is only for female volunteers, so really your options are to volunteer at one of the homes for the dying or at the orphanage."

Matthew and I sit at a rectangular table, in a small blue alcove. Crosses and pictures of Jesus adorn the walls, as well as phrases and pictures I can't identify. The slightly chill, blue tinged air, is a comfortable respite from the unforgiving heat outside. The walls have a feel of cool clay.

"Well, I was hoping to volunteer at the home for mentally disabled men, as the friend who recommended that I come here had volunteered there. I guess I'd like to volunteer at one of the homes for the dying," I say hesitantly.

"Great. I work at Kalighat, and we could use some help," Matthew responds. "The sisters want me to make sure to tell you to be careful of your health. Masks, gloves, and aprons are available for all volunteers. Wearing a mask is important as many of our patients are dying of tuberculosis, which is an airborne disease. You should also be wary of coming into contact with any blood or saliva secretions. If you think you have touched anything dangerous, there is a basin of disinfectant in each home that you can use to clean your hands. You should also be aware that several volunteers have caught malaria and are currently in the hospital. If you have malaria pills, you should be taking them."

"Wow. That sounds scary."

"Don't worry. I mean, it is kind of scary, but I've been here for several months, and except for the malaria, it's been fine. If you wear the mask and gloves, you'll be fine."

"Oh. And, if I do come and volunteer, what are my commitments?"

"You are free to come and go as you wish," Matthew reassures me. "You are never required to come to work, nor are you required to do any kind of service that you don't want to do. The only thing that the sisters ask is that you inform us if you leave Calcutta earlier than planned, so they won't worry about you.

"At the homes for the destitute and dying, help is needed to wash the clothes and serve lunch. Some volunteers give the patients massages or read stories to them, or simply sit with them. Whatever you want to do is fine. All the help we get is important."

"Okay. What time should I come if I want to start tomorrow?"

"There are prayer services at 6:30, which all volunteers are invited to attend. At 7:00 there will be tea and bread for breakfast. We'll head out at 7:30."

"I'd like to see the prayer services."

"That's great. Oh," Matthew adds. "One word of warning. There are some children who may ask you for money. In general, we recommend not giving to any of the beggars you see around here. The mafia controls all the begging in this area, so your money won't go to the person you give to anyway. We feel that if you are going to give, then you are better off giving to the Sisters of Charity, or to some other charitable group who will put the money to good use. If you really want to give something to the children, then we suggest that you buy them some candy. Just make sure that you remove the wrapping, or the child will sell the candy back to the store for money. In the same way, if you want to buy them some milk, make sure that you open the package when you give it to them. Any questions?"

"Not at this moment, but I'm sure I'll think of some later."

"You can always come find me if you want to know something. Okay?"

"Okay. I guess I'll see you tomorrow."

He holds out his hand, and I shake it.

"See you tomorrow."

3.

I arrive at the mission before 6:30, tired, nervous, and curious. A Sister of Charity opens the door and quietly steps aside, allowing me to enter. I find that many people are already here, young men and women from various foreign countries, clustered in small intimate groups, talking animatedly to each other. I don't see Matthew, and I'm too insecure to walk into a group that already seems to know each other and introduce myself, so I walk around and explore. Statements of Christian ideology cover the walls. "Let my hands heal thy broken body." "Let every action of mine be something beautiful for God." "When I was hungry, you gave me to eat. When I was thirsty, you gave me to drink. When I was naked, you clothed me. Whatsoever you do to the least of my brothers, you do unto me." "It is not how much we do, but how much love we put in the doing. It is not how much we give, but how much love we put in the giving."

Pictures of Jesus on the Cross adorn the walls and the stairwell. Mother Theresa's tomb sits in another room, surrounded by praying supplicants. Everywhere I look I see a reminder that I'm an outsider, that when it comes to their fundamental beliefs I do not belong here. I wonder if I'll be able to fit in, or if there will be pressure for me to accept their faith in Jesus. I have no interest in converting, and though I am curious about their beliefs, I want to be accepted for who I am.

At 6:30 most of the volunteers leave the lower floor and walk up a winding stairway. I follow them into a large square room, where a priest and numerous sisters wait quietly. We enter and sit on the floor in the back. Once we have assembled, the priest, standing behind a small podium, begins the mass. "No one knows when the end of the world will be," he says sternly. "When it happens, if you haven't accepted Jesus as your savior, it will be too late!" Now I really feel nervous about being here.

We file out of the room after the mass ends, back down the stairs, and into a room where someone has set out tea, bananas and bread. Volunteers wearing jeans and tee-shirts hang out together in small groups, eating and chatting contentedly. I find myself hovering at their edge, trying to make out the conversation. People see me and smile kindly, but no one invites me over. When I finally spot Matthew, I feel relieved.

"Care for a tour?" he asks.

"That would be great. Thank you."

Matthew walks me around and introduces me to some of the other volunteers. I want to know if the nuns pressure volunteers to convert, but I'm afraid to ask directly. I notice a picture of a train on one of the walls. It doesn't have an obvious religious message, and I think that asking about it might give me an opportunity to assess whether I can voice my concerns to Matthew.

"What is that?" I ask.

"Oh, that." He smiles. "That commemorates the way this all began. Do you know why Mother Theresa began this work?"

"No. I thought maybe the church sent her here."

"Not exactly. Originally, she worked for the church as a teacher, but this changed on September 10, 1946. Mother Theresa was on a train going from Calcutta to Darjeeling, when she heard God's voice, saying 'Feed my poor.' At first, she ignored the words, feeling sure that God couldn't be speaking to her, but when she heard the voice a second time, she knew it was real.

"When she returned to Calcutta, she started helping people she found on the streets. She was by herself, so at first all she could do was to hold them as they died, and tell them that they were loved, that they mattered to God. After some time, she gained a few followers and was able to rent a building and get some beds and clothing.

"She named this center Nirmal Hriday, which means 'pure heart' in Bengali. But we generally call it Kalighat, because it's located next to a very important Hindu temple to the goddess Kali, the goddess of death and destruction. This death and destruction, by the way, is not physical carnage. Kali is supposed to help provide liberation of the soul by destroying the ego and attachment to the physical body. If you think about it, it's a fascinating coincidence – if you believe in coincidence. Both the temple for Kali and Mother Theresa's Kalighat have the same goal – to free people from the mundane world in order to help them reach the sublime. I'm actually writing a poem for my thesis on this subject.

"At any rate, when the Hindu priests discovered that there was a Catholic Sister working next to their holy site, they demanded that the authorities shut her down. They worried that she was helping the poor in order to convert them to Christianity before they died. They feared that she was buying their conversion with food and shelter. They organized protests, which grew louder and angrier until a miracle occurred.

"One day she found a young man lying in the street dying of cholera. The story says that she picked him up with her own hands and carried him to Nirmal Hriday. As was her custom, she bathed him and clothed him in clean clothes, and gave him food and love until he died.

"But this young man was different from the others that she had helped. He was the son of the high priest of Kali's temple. When news of her kindness to the high priest's son spread, opposition to her shelter stopped almost immediately.

"Now that you're here, you'll see the truth of this story. No one is ever turned away from the homes, and no one is pressured to believe what the sisters believe, or to convert."

"Actually, I'm relieved to hear that," I blurt out. "After the service, with all the talk of being saved...I'm Jewish, and I was worried that this might be a problem."

"Well, you should probably expect proselytizing during mass, but if it makes you uncomfortable, you don't have to come. You shouldn't worry about it. Actually, a lot of Israelis come here. The Sisters are very open about their beliefs, but no one will pressure you to conform or convert."

Tension drains from my body. I needed to hear that.

"And what about this?" I ask, pointing to picture of a big heart, within which is inscribed many tiny names.

"Oh," he says, "That's the Immaculate Heart of Mary. Inside that heart are written the names of all the Sisters of Charity who have died. The idea comes from a Catholic belief about Mary, and directly relates to the work that is done here. The belief is that when Jesus was crucified, Mary came to be with him. She couldn't save him or take him off of the cross, but she could be with him so he would die surrounded by his mother's love. And this is what the Sisters of Charity believe they are doing. They are trying to imitate Mary's love. They cannot cure the people they find on Calcutta's streets, but they can show them that they are holy, that their lives have meaning, and that they are loved. It's a beautiful vision, and it's important work. You'll see."

"And what about the signs under the cross that say, 'I thirst?'"

"That's another part of their belief. When Jesus was on the cross, he told Mary that he was thirsty. The belief is that he wasn't thirsty for water, but for souls."

This last comment disturbs me. I feel defensive, like the Hindu priests who opposed Mother Theresa's work. And, from what I know of Catholic beliefs, and indeed, from what I heard the priest say during mass, conversion is a central part of their mission. But I remember my thoughts back in the sannyasin's cage – to try to be open to the good that is before me – and I resolve to at least give myself one full day to experience what this will be like. I can always leave after that.

4.

A twenty-minute bus ride takes us to the section of town where both Kalighat and Kali's temple stand. Small shops selling red hibiscus flowers, animal skulls, sweets, rice, prayer beads and other religious items relating to the temple, as well as pictures of Kali, with her blue skin and four arms, a head in her left hand and a bloody sword in her right, line the side of the road. Unlike elsewhere, the merchants don't try to pull us into their stalls as the items for sale are for religious Hindus and not for foreign tourists.

Nirmal Hriday itself is a non-descript, two-story tall white building, located at the end of the street. I never would have been able to find it without a guide.

The sounds of hundreds of pedestrians and the blare of morning traffic disappear the moment we walk into the small recess behind the doorway. It's very dark, and before my eyes can adjust my nose is assaulted by a pungent smell of decay, defecation and disinfectant. It's suddenly hard to breathe.

I follow the others out of the recess and into the hallway, and I'm confronted by faces of death. Sunken eye sockets stare at me from gaunt faces. Pale flesh, taught parchment-like skin, bones protruding from skinny limbs, countenances of pain, exhaustion and despair, shock me. I've never seen anything like this. The eyes that look at me, the hands that stretch out towards me, terrify me. What am I doing here?

I stare at the floor and try to stay in the middle of the crowd.

But people disperse and head off to their tasks, leaving me exposed. I look around, panicked, until I spot Matthew, standing in a flimsy white smock, lost in thought. I rush towards him.

"What do I do?" I ask, breathless.

"Come here," he says, leading me mercifully away from the rows of patient beds. "The first thing you should know is how to protect yourself. We keep the smocks, gloves, and masks in this cabinet. You probably want to put these on before you go back into the patient area. And here," we turn around and walk to an alcove which contains a basin of clear liquid, "is the disinfectant. If you ever touch something and don't know what it is, wash right away with this. It's better to be careful than not, so use it whenever you think you should.

"Now, there are two main chores that need to be done. I'm going back to the patient area, back by the entrance, to help wash and feed the patients. If you want, you can come back there with me and I'll show you what to do. Or, you can go in here," he leads me to a large open room behind the alcove, "and help wash the patients' clothing and bed sheets."

The washing area is a spacious, square room, filled with healthy, smiling volunteers. They stand in a circle, talking and laughing as they wring water out of wet blue bed sheets. In the back corner, a few people grasp long wooden poles, which they use to stir large vats of liquid, while in another area, two Japanese girls stomp on wet clothing that lies on the ground. The air, moist and damp, is relatively free of the smell of death and decay which pervades the other area and, most importantly, the room is completely free of dying people.

"I think I'll try helping out here for now," I say, trying to sound nonchalant.

"Great. See that large man over there?" he points towards a man wearing overalls, standing at the head of a large circle of people. I nod my head. "He'll tell you what to do."

I leave Matthew and walk towards the bald, laughing man Matthew indicated. "Matthew said I should ask you how I can help," I blurt out nervously. Water drips from a heavy looking wet blanket, which he holds in his large hairy hands, as he looks me over. "You look like you could use some upper body work," he says with a smile. "Why don't you help us wring out the wet clothes?"

I nod my head and walk in the direction he indicated.

"You can help us," a smiling Asian man says. "I'm Paul." He shakes my hand.

"Jason."

"Nice to meet you. Grab something from that basket of wet laundry and wring it out until you've gotten most of the heavy moisture out of it. When you're satisfied, put it in one of these baskets. Someone will take these to the roof and hang them up outside so they can dry completely, so don't worry if it's still damp when you put it in the basket."

"Thanks." I smile hesitantly, and take out a wet sheet. People stand in a loose circle and chat as they douse the grey concrete floor with water from the washed clothes. I stand among them and do my best to fit in. Everyone seems to be happy, and I tell myself that there is nothing wrong with this work – we are all contributing to the same good cause – but, the truth is, I'm embarrassed to be here. I didn't come to Calcutta to wash clothes. I came to work with the dying, like my friend back home – to touch and be touched. I'm in this room, doing laundry, because I can't bear to look at the patients, and I'm ashamed of my cowardice.

That evening, as I eat dinner, alone, in a nearby restaurant, I wonder what I'm doing in Calcutta. I could be in Shimla, spending time with friends and teaching English during the day, which would still be a type of service. Why did I insist on coming here?

Because, I remind myself, I want to learn how to serve selflessly. My trip was inspired, in part, by a book called *The Miracle of Love*. In the book, Neem Karoli Baba, the Indian guru the stories were about, often spoke of selfless service as a method to get close to God. I know from my own experience that when I serve there are always selfish motives behind my actions. Either I feel obligated to help, in which case I often feel resentful about my service, or I help because I want to do so, in which case I feel good about myself. Either way, I am serving others through selfish motives. But there must be a higher level. A level where service is done because someone needs help, where my own needs don't enter into the equation. I know that my life has to be meaningful in order for it to be fulfilling. Learning selfless service might be a doorway into a life connected with something larger than myself, something greater than my individual needs.

Dorje told me that Calcutta was, "the worst place in the world," and he may be right. But I know that the only way I'll be able to grow into the person I dream of being - a person who's not afraid to give, or love, or be loved - is to keep on showing up and trying. When a child learns to walk, he will fall down repeatedly, but he won't give up. He'll pick himself up and try again.

Tomorrow, I'll return to the mission, and try again. Maybe, one day, I'll find I can look those dying patients in the eye without running away.

5.

Father O'Toole, a priest connected to Mother Theresa's order, offers to meet with volunteers once a week. I'm told that the meeting is to allow us to share our experiences and difficulties with each other, and I want to know if other volunteers are struggling – to endure the smells, to look patients in the eye – as much as I am. Though I know I need to go, I have reservations. I'm worried that this meeting might be a covert attempt to proselytize and convert us.

My fears prove to be well founded. For most of the meeting Father O'Toole debates a young Irish man, born a Catholic, but now a Buddhist, on whether impermanence or Jesus is the true path of a holy life. I came to talk about practical issues, to find out how people cope with touching the dying. I don't want someone to tell me how to live my life, and I don't think any one person or religion has a monopoly on truth.

My meditation teacher tells us that we should evaluate the meditation practice on the basis of whether it improves our lives. If it makes our lives better, he said, we should continue the practice. If it does not, we should stop. I think that this simple rule could and should be applied to any belief system. If a religious practice helps people grow and give and love, then it is valuable. If a religious practice separates good men from each other, or causes harm to people who are trying to grow and give and love, then it is harmful. The extent to which Buddhism or Catholicism or any other religion helps or hinders people's ability to grow and love each other is the extent to which I believe it is useful – and this usefulness could well vary from person to person, or from group to group, as not every practice or belief is understood or utilized in the same way. I desperately wish that the Father and this young Buddhist man would share with us how their beliefs or practices help them to be with the dying. This kind of sharing would be helpful to me. This could help me grow into the person I long to be. Unfortunately, they are both too eager to convince everyone that they have found the true path to salvation to bother listening to each other, or anyone else, and their heated debate drowns out any opportunity the rest of us might have had to learn and connect.

But my coming does prove to be beneficial, despite the fact that the meeting does not meet my expectations. At the end of the 'discussion', Father O'Toole relates a few ideas that help me find my way in Calcutta.

"Why are you here?" Father O'Toole asks. "Why do we invite foreigners to come here and volunteer and serve? To understand this, you have to understand both the lives that our patients have lived and also what you represent to them. They are the Untouchables. Taught from birth that they are beneath all the other castes. They are called Untouchables because they are literally untouchable by the other castes. If by some chance someone from a higher caste does touch them, then this touch makes them impure. Even to look at them is defiling. So, all their lives, the Untouchables have learned that they are beneath other human beings.

"You, on the other hand, are like gods to them. You are mostly light-skinned, which connotes higher status, and you come from foreign countries. To them, you are rich, educated, and free. You have lived lives that they could never even dream of. You are the ideal, the class that has always stepped over them, that has always been too pure to even look at them.

"So, when you come here, when you serve them, when you bring them a glass of water, or touch their hands, you are sending them an incredible message. Their lives do matter. They are not dirty. They are worthy of being loved. The fact that you, someone who comes from Paradise, would come here to serve them – it turns their whole world upside down. Suddenly, they can experience the fact that they are worthy of love. That God loves them. That their existence has meaning and worth."

Father O'Toole follows this story by explaining Mother Theresa's vision, how she saw her mission and her work. "Once, a reporter from the West came here," he says. "And he asked her this question. 'What you do seems very beautiful. You find people on the street who are dying and alone, and you take them in, feed them, clothe them, and try to love them before they die. But, in doing this, you are ignoring the larger issues of class discrimination and poverty, issues which have condemned these people to die, alone, on the streets of Calcutta. Why don't you use your influence to try to change the system that abuses these people?'

"Mother Theresa waited patiently as the reporter launched his attack." Father O'Toole continues. "And when he had finished, she responded simply. 'Do you think it is important to try to change the system here in India,' she asked. 'Yes!' responded the reporter. 'Good,' Mother Theresa said. 'Then you do it. It is important and it should be done. If you feel called to this task, if you are passionate about it, then you go and do it. I am doing this. This is my work. It is not possible for one person to confront every issue in this world. The fact is that people are dying on the streets here. I want them to face God knowing that they were loved. This is important work, and it is my calling. If fighting the poverty in India is your calling, then do it. I am doing this.'"

Mother Theresa's confidence inspires me. She knew what her job was. She knew where she wanted to put her effort and her love, and she dedicated her life to that task. She didn't condemn herself for the things she didn't do, but valued her accomplishments and her mission.

At this moment, I am unable to work with the dying directly. But there's no reason to condemn myself for this. My job at this moment is to accept what I can and cannot do. At the same time, I want to keep working on myself, keep trying to get into that room with the dying. I cannot do everything, but I am going to try to do this.

6.

The entranceway to Kalighat opens directly in front of a long corridor, which contains two crowded rows of beds, with an empty aisle between them. Above the beds, are wooden rafters and arched, open windows, through which thin streams of light often shine through, dully illuminating the grim scene. On the second day, I make a concerted effort to look at the patient area. I force myself to acknowledge the emaciated, awkward, slumping bodies, and the sunken-eyed stares, before hurrying off to the laundry room. On the third day, I slow myself down, and look at the patients more carefully. Their dark, deep-set eyes and taut, bony limbs still frighten me, but it's not as shocking as it was. The odor of decaying bandages and bloody wounds, mixed with the acrid smell of bleach, no longer overwhelms me, and the coldness that gripped my stomach has largely gone away. I no longer feel an urgent need to run from the room.

I decide that I'm ready to at least know what the other volunteers are doing, so I pause in the main room to watch. Patients who can walk, slowly make their way to the back of the room, where they disrobe and walk into another room, returning a few minutes later, wet and shivering, to towel off. As they shower, volunteers remove the bed sheets from the vacant beds, and wash the plastic blue mattresses. Meanwhile, other volunteers prepare to serve breakfast by placing pots of food on a table. I consider trying to help serve breakfast, but I'm still too afraid to get close to the dying residents. I return to the laundry room for another day.

By the fourth day, however, I'm feeling brave. I take a deep breath, steel myself, and remain in the patients' room.

It's easy to spot the people who know what they're doing. Experienced volunteers are compassion in motion, getting needed food, advising or directing less experienced volunteers, sitting next to the patients while lovingly holding their hands as they speak. Two men in particular stand out; one Indian and the other Japanese. If a patient shits himself, they jump to clean it up. If a man is dying, they are at his side to help him face the pain and the unknown. I've never seen people like them, and I hope that some of their spirit and courage will rub off on me.

I take a plastic smock and plastic gloves from the cabinet and put them on before walking over to the table where volunteers have begun to serve bananas, muesli and tea for this morning's breakfast. I ask the Indian man I admire what I can do to help, and he instructs me to feed a short, skinny man lying on a bed in the middle of the dormitory.

I take a plate of food and a cup of coffee complexioned tea from the servers and walk over to the man's bed. The sound of metal spoons scraping metal bowls, and the din of conversation and chewing fills the air. The man sits up when I approach and eagerly opens his toothless mouth, waiting breathlessly for some food. His head and his gaping mouth look gigantic compared to his severely emaciated body. I pick up a spoonful of muesli, mix it with some tea as I see other volunteers do, and direct the spoon towards his mouth. His whole body shakes in anticipation and his mouth and gums open so wide it nearly cracks his face in half. I'm afraid he's going to swallow my hand.

He closes his gums over the spoon and the food slides inside. As soon as I withdraw the spoon from his mouth, he begins to scream in English, "More! More! More!" Food flies out of his mouth and a rivulet of brown tea drips down his chin as he shouts at me.

As quickly as I can, I put another spoonful into his mouth. Still he yells at me. "More! Babu. More!"

I start to panic, and I feed him as fast as I can. Bits of muesli and banana fall out of his slobbering mouth, onto his clothes and onto the floor. He's so desperate that he hardly chews what he's given. Saliva and tea are everywhere, and I'm grateful that I'm wearing the smock and gloves.

In a matter of minutes, the plate and cup are empty. "More! More!" He cries out, hands outstretched, pleading, reaching out to me and to anyone who will listen. I stand up quickly and try to reassure him that I'll return in a moment with more food. As I turn to go a volunteer stops me. He looks over my shoulder at the skinny man with a mixture of pity and humor in his eyes.

"He's always hungry," he tells me. "I think he wants to die by eating. Don't give him anymore. He has bad diarrhea. If he eats too much he'll get sick. We'll have to clean him up and he'll feel miserable."

I turn back to look at the man and see that his eyes are filled with hate. He may not understand English, but he knows what I've been told. He snorts at us in disgust and begins shouting at other volunteers. "More! Babu. More!"

I turn away from the patient and try to stop my arms from shaking. I return the dirty tray to the servers' table, take off my gloves, and hurry to the laundry room where I understand the rules and no one tries to trick me into killing them with food.

7.

When I grab a tray of food the next day, I hope to get the same guy. Serving him without allowing him to freak me out will go a long way toward helping me recover from yesterday's ordeal. Unfortunately, another volunteer is already feeding him so I'm directed to a pale, sour-looking man. I sit next to him and put spoonfuls of food into his mouth. He eats slowly, painfully, as if each bite he swallows requires concentration and effort. He doesn't complain and doesn't communicate. He simply opens his mouth, chews his food and waits for the next bite.

I finish feeding him, place the cup, bowl, and spoon in an area reserved for dirty dishes and look around to see what I can do next. A few men shuffle slowly toward the back of the room. They march as if being led to prison, reluctantly placing one foot in front of the other, heads hanging low, shoulders slumped dejectedly. They are required to bathe every day, but that doesn't mean they're happy about it. On the other hand, at least they can transport themselves.

"Can you help me with him," a stocky volunteer from Australia points to a tall man lying in a bed to his left.

"Sure," I reply.

"We need to carry him to the showers," he says. "See if you can grab his legs."

I look down at the man. He's so thin that I've actually seen him wrap his middle finger and thumb around his thigh. He turns his ashen face away as we approach, and I realize it's an affront to his dignity to be carried. I'm uneasy about subjecting him to this embarrassment, but I know that if we don't clean the patients this place will be overrun by disease.

I grab the man's legs and the other volunteer wraps his arms around the man's thin chest. I'm not a big guy, so I prepare to strain to lift him, but I'm shocked to discover I can pick him up with ease. This six foot tall man can't weigh much more than a hundred pounds.

We carry him to the back of the room, where three naked men, bare feet on the cold grey floor, rib cages extruding from emaciated torsos, await their turn to shower. They stand, shivering, amidst dusty streams of light, which tentatively illuminates the dim and depressing scene, and watch as we gently place our charge on an empty blue mattress and undress him. His grey chest hairs appear fragile; his skin is like cracked parchment. We throw his dirty clothes into a pile and carefully carry him into the showers. The Indian man who I admire is here, kneeling on the ground and washing a prone figure with a large soapy sponge.

He smiles up at us. "Put him down over there," he nods towards an empty patch of floor. "I'll be with him in a moment."

The shower area is a square, grey and white, concrete box, with rows of showerheads protruding from the walls. Shivering, wet men stand in the room, washing themselves as quickly as possible. The water is freezing cold, and no one has even a shred of privacy. With the exception of the Indian volunteer, whose eyes are bright with love, everyone looks like they want to scream and cry. I put the man down, walk past the naked men, and run back to the safety of the laundry area. I'll try to do more tomorrow.

8.

Each day, I push my boundaries one small step at a time. Feeding patients soon becomes part of my routine, as does helping carry men to the showers. I find that the more I participate and the more I'm exposed to these men, their appearance and their personalities, the less frightening they become. The first man I helped feed asks for food all day long. Another will spit his medicine at the wall when the volunteer leaves his side. Yet another, once an English teacher, is generally too weak to say more than a word or two, but always smiles and says "thank you" when we help him. The undifferentiated mass of suffering gives way to individuated needs, and the more they become individuals, the easier it is to know how to help.

After a week, I no longer have to ask for directions but can take a look around and decide for myself what needs to be done. I discover that I've become one of the volunteers who knows the routine. New people come to me for instructions. I'm proud of myself. In less than two weeks, I find that I've uncovered a dormant reserve of compassion and love. I feel like I've become a peer of the Indian and Japanese men who lead the volunteers, and I start to believe that the transformation I was looking for, that the person I hoped I could be has begun to emerge. This pride lasts until I'm confronted with my first acutely dying person.

9.

The severity of patients' illnesses determines their place in the patient area. Those closer to the front are closer to death. Two beds in the very front of the room are reserved for people whose death is imminent. For the first week, these beds are empty and I learn to ignore them. But now, into my second week, the English teacher lies in one of them.

I help feed and wash the patients as usual, occasionally glancing towards him. He has no energy, moves listlessly, moans softly in his sleep. But there comes a moment when I look over and the English teacher, frightened and agonized with pain, wakes up and reaches out a hand towards me. I stagger backward, as if his hand was the touch of death itself. What does he want with me? Is he about to die?

My secure inner world collapses. I whirl around, spot the Indian volunteer that I admire, and race to him for help.

"Look!" I shout, grabbing his arm and pointing at the man in the bed. "He needs something."

The young volunteer doesn't hesitate. With one swift, fluid motion, he is at the patient's bedside. Kneeling beside the bed, he grabs the man's outstretched hand, then strokes the man's head with his free hand, and looks compassionately into his eyes. The old man sinks back down into the bed, still frightened, but comforted to no longer be alone.

I'm ashamed. A dying man reached out to me, looking for a hand to hold, and I ran for help.

When I arrived in Calcutta, I had an idea that selfless service, selfless love might exist. Now that I've had a chance to observe volunteers at

Kalighat, I see that it does exist. That Indian man never hesitates to help people in need. He never worries about how the patients look or how they smell, he simply sits with them and cares for them and loves them.

Everything about this center has been difficult to deal with; the awful smells, the dying men, my own fears and prejudices. But each day I get a little more acclimated and things that were too horrible to bear witness to become easier to be near. I want to be able to accompany these people into the unknown. I want to be able to sit with them with love and compassion, without being frightened away by their pain. To do so I know I have to continue to show up and try. This, I remind myself, has been the secret. To push myself a little more each day. To keep on trying, even after repeated failures. And I will keep on trying, until, hopefully, one morning I will discover that I too have uncovered the depth of love it takes to respond to a stranger in need, without worrying, or thinking, or fearing, but simply by responding as I know is necessary.

Over the next few days, the English teacher recovers. Soon, he is back at his old bed, and he laughs and chats with us with renewed energy. I watch him carefully, looking to see if he is judging me or is disappointed in me. I feel embarrassed, and I want to apologize, but he gives no sign of ill will towards me, and I decide to let it pass. This is my problem. There's no need to burden him with my need for forgiveness, nor to make him remember that frightening moment when he was so near to death, and I was too scared to give him comfort.

10.

I keep my eyes open as I go about my routine, looking for opportunities to step forward and offer someone personal help. I want to challenge myself. I want to step out of my comfort zone, but we are undermanned, and it is all we can do just to get the washing and the meals accomplished.

Unfortunately, after only a couple of days of feeling well the teacher returns to the front bed, pale and weak. He can swallow only a few mouthfuls of food, and is too fragile to be washed. I watch him with concern as I go about my daily routine, and when the day is almost over, the man reaches out to me again. This time I don't hesitate. I stride over to him, take his hand, kneel down and put my free hand on his forehead.

He's hot to touch. He grabs a hold of my hand and pulls it to his chest. My heart beats wildly. It's hard to breathe. What should I do? What does he need? I stroke his forehead, like I saw the Indian volunteer do, and murmur, "You're not alone. I'm here. You're not alone." I feel awkward and useless, but something is happening. He convulses once or twice, stares at the ceiling in terror, and grabs my hand with all his might, but when the spasm passes, he leans back, relaxes slightly, sinks slowly into his bed.

His shuddering, infrequent breaths pulsate through my body. His face is clenched in pain and fear. When he opens his eyes, the whites stare outward as his eyelids are pushed up as far as they can go.

I stroke his forehead occasionally, but mostly I just sit by him and hold his hand. As time passes, I let go of my anxiety. It suddenly seems clear that holding his hand, simply being with him as he faces his death, is the most important thing I can do. I cannot stop him from dying, but I can stop him from dying alone.

By the time the morning shift ends, the man is almost asleep. His eyelids droop and the grip on my hand loosens. The lines of his face relax, his body sags, and the terror in his eyes recedes. The spasm of pain or fear that racked his body has ended. I gently remove my hand from his grip, lay a light kiss on his forehead, and leave the building.

When the sunlight hits me, I almost fall over. My body begins to shake and my limbs feel like rubber. I want to cry. I never knew it was possible to really be with someone who was suffering. Always before there was something to do – feed the patients, wash them, dispense medicine, clean the clothes or dishes – but when that man was in pain what he needed was someone to be there with him. And that someone was me. And my being there was more important than all the actions I had undertaken for the past two weeks. I don't know what it's like to feel death painfully and inexorably moving through one's body, but I do know, now, how comforting it can be not to have to face that alone. I held his hand, and that made all the difference.

11.

Working at the Mother Theresa Mission is challenging enough, but Sudder Street, the tourist area near the mission where most of the volunteers live, poses its own set of difficulties. During the day, children, mothers holding crying babies, and old men in threadbare clothing beg for food and money. The longer I live here, the more despair I feel over my inability to find a comfort zone, or decide how to react to the misery I see.

My first response was to pick one person and try to help him or her, but this has proven to be unsatisfactory. Inevitably, the recipient of my charity will inspect my donation quickly, look up at me and begin shouting that it's not enough. I've also tried buying one of the beggars some food, but this also becomes embarrassing and upsetting. They appear grateful for the invitation, but as they eat, they complain about the quality of the food, making sure I know that I'm not doing enough. I know of other people who have bought the beggars blankets or clothing from nearby stores, only to discover later that the beggars have sold the item back to the store. My guilt is compounded by my inability to do anything to alleviate even a small portion of it.

Two events in particular challenge me to reevaluate the situation and attitude of the people on Sudder Street. One day an especially aggressive woman accosts Miri, a petite volunteer from Switzerland, and myself. The woman holds a screaming baby in one hand, while her other arm stretches out towards us, holding an empty milk bottle.

"Milk, please. For baby," she cries, blocking our path with her body.

We happen to be standing right in front of Miri's hotel, which gives her an idea.

"Let me have the bottle," she says, reaching out for it. "I'll get you some milk from inside."

"No," the woman pulls back the bottle. "From the store."

"It's okay," Miri persists. "I can get you some milk. Don't worry. I'll bring the bottle back."

"No!" The woman shakes her head furiously. "Not here. From store." Her baby shrieks in desperation. Giant, heavy sobs shake its' little body.

"Come on," Miri demands, getting angry now. "Let me have the bottle."

For a moment they stare at each other, locked in a strange battle of wills. We have been told that the mafia runs this street, and that everyone begging here works for them, but what does that have to do with hungry children and desperate mothers? Whatever it is, Miri is threatening to expose it. She is confident, commanding. Her outstretched arm is both an offer of help and a threat. Either allow her to fill the bottle with milk or quit pretending that that's what you need.

The young woman's angry look dissolves into resignation, and she hands Miri the bottle.

"I'll be right back," Miri says. She walks into the hotel, leaving me with the woman and the baby, who is now strangely quiet.

We stare at each other. I smile at the woman, trying to demonstrate that I'm a friend. Look, I care. I'm smiling. She scowls at me in return.

A few minutes later, Miri returns with a full milk bottle. The woman snatches the bottle out of Miri's hand with a quick, violent gesture, glares at us bitterly, and storms away.

This episode makes absolutely no sense to me until I discuss it with Matthew at the mission the next day. "Those babies are rented from women who live in nearby villages." He tells me. "The women carrying them around the street are not their mothers. It's all an act to try to get tourists' money. If you watch closely, you may catch them pinching the baby's behind. They know they'll get more money if the baby is crying.

What she wanted was money, not milk. If you bought her milk from a store, she could return the box for money. When you filled the baby's bottle, not only doesn't she get any money, but she has to wash out the bottle before she can continue to beg. You probably ruined her day."

Later, I hear a story that, again, makes me wonder about the relationship between the beggars and well-meaning tourists. A middle-aged man from Belgium tells me about a woman he met begging on Sudder Street. Even though they didn't share a common language, she managed to tell him about her newborn baby girl, about her unreliable husband, and about their struggles to survive in their poor village. He felt that a bond had formed between them, and he decided to try to do something to change her life. His idea was to open a bank account in her name and put enough money into it so that she could keep the principle intact and use the interest to purchase things that her family would need. In the future, when her daughter was grown, she could use the principle to pay for her education or her dowry.

Opening a bank account for an illiterate peasant woman was more difficult than he had imagined. First, the minimum amount of money needed to open a bank account was $250. As this was the average yearly income in India, it probably represented more money than this woman, who subsisted on begging, ever would have seen in her lifetime. It was also more than he originally wanted to give, but he was determined to do something to change this woman's life.

Even when he decided that the amount of money was not an obstacle, he still had many challenges to overcome. To open the account he had to travel to the woman's remote village, hire a translator, and take the woman, her husband, and the translator to the bank so they could open the account together. As is usual in India, everything took longer and was more complicated than he expected. It took an entire day of haggling, arguing, and hassle to open the account for his friend. He persevered, and by the time the bank closed, he had been successful.

As they left the bank, he tried to explain to her, through his translator, his idea that she should leave the principle intact and use only the interest.

In this way she would have a sort of income and would have the balance in reserve for an emergency or for her daughter's future.

She listened politely until he finished speaking. Then she explained that her house needed repairs. Could he pay for it? It wouldn't be much money and she really needed the help.

He was stunned. He had traveled to her village. He had hired an interpreter. He had spent the day fighting with the bank manager to get him to open an account for her when she was too illiterate to even sign her name. He had given her a lot of money. Now, instead of thanks, she wanted more.

The more I experience this hostility, the more I wonder about the strangeness of it all. Why do they dismiss our attempts to help them? Why are they never satisfied? Over time, I think I understand.

When I lived in New York City, I bore witness to its' homeless problem. Countless people sat on street corners, a battered paper cup by their side, begging for spare change. Old men and women walked around with stolen grocery carts filled with the odds and ends of their lives. They paused to dive into garbage cans, searching for recyclable loot. Many people slept in subway stations and on street corners, shivering under cardboard boxes and filthy blankets. It was painful to witness, and I eventually decided that if I couldn't help everyone, perhaps I could focus the little I could do on one person.

There was a homeless man named John that I would pass on my way to and from school. He would smile kindly, and say thank you with humility whenever I gave him a dollar. This became part of my daily routine, and as the days went by he came to recognize me. One day, he opened up to me. His brother thought he was a bum. People on the street harassed him and sometimes robbed him. He had dreams of becoming a janitor and moving out of the city.

For twenty minutes I stood in the cold as a slight flurry of snowflakes fell around us, listening to John's sad story, silently wondering when he'd stop talking and I could go home. After that day, whenever I passed by he wanted to talk to me. In his mind, we had become friends.

I found myself facing an awful dilemma. I didn't want to take twenty minutes out of my commute every day to speak to this man. I had things to do and these interruptions took precious time from my life. Besides, this was getting dangerous. What if he wanted more from me than a dollar and a look in the eye? What if he wanted me to become involved in his life?

I discovered, sadly, that my kindness had been a ruse. I wanted to try to do something nice for John, but there was a limit. I didn't want to take on his sadness and his problems. He needed a friend, and this was more than I wanted to offer.

There didn't seem to be any way to go back to the simpler days when I could give him a dollar, feel good about myself, and walk away. I changed my route so as to avoid the areas where John hung out. I felt guilty about it, but what he needed was more than I was prepared to give.

It occurs to me that my situation here is very similar. I feel guilt when I see Sudder Street's beggars, and I want this guilt to go away. More than that, I want to be able to tell myself that I'm a good person. Look, I want to say, I gave that person twenty rupees. Aren't I nice?

But what if the beggars here have had experiences like my experience with John in New York City? What if they saw the apparent kindness of foreigners and tried to become friends with them? What if they found out, like John did, that the money they were given, merely a pittance from the standpoint of the rich visitors, was not an offer of friendship, but instead was meant to purchase freedom from feelings of guilt? This might explain their hostility. They see through the illusion that we wish to create. They know that deep down we do feel superior, even when we pretend that we don't. They know that deep down we want to feel that we deserve what we have and that they probably deserve what they have. I think that if we didn't think that way, it would be truly unbearable to see their suffering. How can I watch someone sleep on the cold streets and walk on by unless I imagine that they somehow are responsible for their situation, that they wasted the chances that they had, or that they never really had the potential to succeed in life? It's not pleasant to think these thoughts, but they might be true. Certainly, I think that they are true for me. But knowing the truth doesn't always change it. Not unless I want it to change. And I don't.

I remember Mother Theresa's wisdom. I came here to work in the Homes for the Destitute and Dying. I didn't come here to combat India's immense poverty. I wish I could do more, but I have limitations. What little of myself that I have to give, I'm giving at the homes.

12.

Of all the homes that Mother Theresa established in Calcutta, by far the one that is the most mysterious and the most frightening to me is the Leper Colony. Volunteers are not invited to work there, but every two weeks the mission offers the opportunity to visit the site. I have seen lepers since I've been to India, and their condition horrifies me. I don't know how I'll react to an entire settlement. Other volunteers, however, have told me that I can't miss visiting the colony, that the Brothers of Charity who run it perform a miracle there. I'm curious to see this miracle, but I'm also afraid. The first week that I'm in Calcutta there's an opportunity to go, but I manage to forget about it. Miri, my courageous friend, does not forget and returns from her visit so excited that she can hardly stand still. "It was so beautiful," she tells me. "The lepers smiled and laughed like children. It's truly amazing. It would be a shame if you missed it."

Her eyes radiate warmth and happiness, and I want to experience this feeling. After working for the past three weeks at Kalighat, I finally think I'm ready to visit the colony. I hope that having learned to see beyond the physical condition of the dying patients at Kalighat I will be able to see the people behind the lepers' decaying flesh.

In order to get to the leper colony, we have to take a local train. Because the train begins in Calcutta, it's empty when we board. Unfortunately, hundreds of people board with us, so two minutes after the doors open we find ourselves scrunched to the point of suffocation between a multitude of Indian men and women. Somehow, as the train moves from station to station, we manage to take on even more passengers as people push themselves into the car, hang out of the windows, and hold onto the outside of the door. At every stop there's an earthquake of rough pushing and shoving as some people attempt to disembark while others desperately try to push themselves aboard. It's a claustrophobic, smelly – think 100 degree heat and no deodorant – nightmare. Our saving grace is that the leper colony is way out in the countryside. By the time we arrive enough people have disembarked so that we can squirm free.

A five-minute walk past rolling green hills, under a vast blue-sky, leads us to the gates of the colony. When we enter, a pair of young giggling women greet us. All the way to the colony, I have been bracing myself to face images of people suffering from a horrible, degenerative disease. I'm totally unprepared for mirth and laughter.

At first, because of their laughter, I assume that these women are not lepers. Maybe they're just young girls who work here? But they raise their hands to cover their mouths as they laugh, and their disfigured fingers dispel any doubt as to who they are.

The two women, giggling like excited schoolgirls, lead us to the main office. As we walk down the dirt path, past rows of flowerbeds, they point to our cameras and pose for pictures, or reach out to hold hands with the women in our group. Their joy completely outshines their deformities. I have to remind myself that they are lepers, that they are living in a leper colony, that they are here because they contracted one of the world's most awful diseases. I'm supposed to feel sorry for them. But their laughter is infectious. I smile and laugh along with them, though I have no idea what we're laughing about.

They lead us to a small, one-story building, which contains the offices of the Brothers of Charity. The wood paneled walls match the simple brown of the brother's robes. A tall, white-haired brother nods politely in our direction and thanks the two ladies for bringing us to him. They walk away, still laughing.

"My name is Brother John," he says in a gentle, soft voice – the voice of someone used to giving comfort. "Thank you for coming to visit us today. The work that you do in the various homes in Calcutta is invaluable to us and to the people you serve. You have become part of our family by working with us, and we want to share with you the work we do in this center.

"Although we don't know how leprosy is contracted, we do know that a person's immune system has to be severely depleted before they can contract the disease. This is why only the poorest of the poor, all over the world, get leprosy. As you are all healthy and well-nourished, none of you have to worry about contracting leprosy while you visit here.

"Because we don't know how the disease is spread, we can't prevent it, but we can cure it. Sometimes a volunteer or a member of our order will discover someone with leprosy in the streets of Calcutta. Other times, people with leprosy will hear about our center and will come on their own. Naturally, it's our mission to cure anyone who comes here for free.

"Once cured, our patients have two options available to them. We invite and encourage everyone we cure to stay here and become a part of the community. If they wish, however, they are free to go back to the communities that they came from.

"One thing you may notice is that the people who live here constantly hold each other's hands. According to Hindu belief, leprosy is a curse from the gods. Once the first signs of decay appear, their families and friends abandon them. Husbands separate from wives and children are taken away from their parents. They become literally untouchable, discarded by everyone they have ever known or loved, cursed forever by the gods.

"In this place, however, this stigma does not exist. People are free to rediscover the pleasure of simple human touch. Some of our residents even remarry and start new lives.

"Today you have the opportunity to walk through the different facets of life here. We'll visit the clinic where our patients get treatment. And we'll visit the farmland, the weaving room, and the school, so you can get a sense of the community that our residents have built."

We exit the building, and follow Brother John through lush green meadows, past gardens of beautiful flowers, into barns filled with cows and chickens. All around us ex-lepers smile and laugh and pose for pictures. Many of them are holding hands, still grateful for the sense of human contact which leprosy had taken away from them. I've never seen people so at ease, so joyous, so eager to be touched and seen. I'm envious of their happiness.

My enthusiasm is tempered by our visit to the treatment facility. Indian people, dark beside their coverings of white bandages, scream at us with their eyes. Their hands are mere stumps. Their arms and legs have twisted and grown grotesque. This is what I expected to see. People trapped in visibly deteriorating bodies, wounded by the horror of their own decay. I can only imagine what terror hides beneath their bandages. The fact that no one knows how the disease spreads chills me. I understand why their loved ones send them away. Fear of contracting such a disease would drive away anyone but a saint, and those who contracted such a disease would know the deepest meaning of being alone.

After the treatment facility, we visit the colony's school; a one-room classroom with desks and a blackboard, filled with energetic, healthy, leprosy free, children of all ages. The lone schoolteacher, a very skinny woman in a plain white button down shirt and a blue skirt, raps her wooden pointer against the blackboard to silence her young charges, but our presence causes too great a disturbance. The children run around us, scream and yell, grab our hands, and laugh. After a few minutes of fruitlessly banging her stick on the board, the teacher shrugs her shoulders and gives up. We watch the chaos for a while, grateful to see all this vibrant life after visiting the treatment center. When our guide takes us out of the room, the children run and scream after us, until the teacher's loud yell drags them, reluctantly, back into the classroom.

It's both a surprise and a relief to see that lepers can have healthy, normal children. This in itself feels like some sort of cleansing – a victory of life.

Lastly, we visit the weaving room. Here, again, I see the painful triumph of life over disease. Some of the cured lepers who retain use of their hands learn how to use looms. Here they make the blue and white uniforms for the Sisters of Charity, as well as blankets, sheets, and even backpacks, which they sell to make money for the center. The women operating the looms smile happily at us as we pass. Many have bandages wrapped around their hands, but despite their deformities, they work the levers and manipulate the thread quickly and efficiently.

"With the food we grow, with what the animals produce, and with the products that these women weave, we have been able to build a self-sufficient community," Brother John continues. "We have helped them build a society where they can live, touch, and love without the continuing stigma of having once contracted leprosy. We are quite proud of what we have accomplished together. I hope that after walking the grounds with me, you understand why. Thank you for coming. Thank you for the work that you do."

As I leave the leper colony, as the image of Brother John's compassion lingers in my mind, I think I understand the difference between pity and compassion, between the beggars' hostility to me and the patients' love. The Brothers of Charity have compassion for the lepers. They live among them and dedicate their lives to really changing the circumstances in which they live. In a similar manner, I show compassion for the patients at Kalighat by giving them my time and effort. True compassion requires a willingness to make personal sacrifices in order to help another person. When I contrast this to how I react to the beggars on the street; namely that I pity them, give them money and walk on by, I better understand the beggars' attitude. The fact is, I shouldn't expect the beggars to respond to me as the patients do. They have a right to feel resentful when they see I'm giving to others, while effectively neglecting their plight, as if the people in the homes have value, while they do not. Understanding things in this way doesn't make Sudder Street less difficult for a healthy, rich, foreigner to walk through, but it does keep me from judging the beggars too harshly when they resent my presence and money.

I'm also developing a true appreciation for the resiliency of life – both within myself and within others. The people at the leper colony largely seem to have rebounded from one of the most horrible diseases in the world. When given a second chance at life, they were able to take it and thrive. I imagine that they overcame their pain and fear in exactly the way I have been able to overcome obstacles at Kalighat – simply by trying, day by day, and getting up and trying again whenever they failed. It may be that as long as we don't give up trying, we can eventually learn how to make any situation better – this may be how we heal, even from seemingly impossible pain.

13.

When I first arrived, there were only six men working in the patient area, and we needed to race from one task to the next, but as Christmas nears, additional volunteers arrive, and soon there is insufficient work to keep all of us occupied. The problem peaks when a group of fifteen men, on leave from the French Armed Forces, come to volunteer. Suddenly we have more than thirty volunteers serving thirty patients. One day I am an essential member of the team and the next I stand around looking for something to do.

Over lunch I complain to my friend Sergio who volunteers at Prem Dam (Bengali for Gift of Love), the other home for the dying, located in a different part of Calcutta. He's astonished. "We have 200 men at Prem Dam and only six volunteers to do the work. I'm completely exhausted. If you're bored at Kalighat, why don't you come with me tomorrow and work with us? We're desperate for some more help."

He warns me that the work is very hard. Some of patients are visibly handicapped, and many can't take care of themselves at all.

After my experiences at Kalighat, after watching myself grow from a person who could only stand to do the laundry to someone who could hold the hand of a dying man, I feel I can handle anything. "No problem," I tell him confidently and, as it turns out, foolishly.

Prem Dam instantly overwhelms me. Bed pans, overflowing with urine and shit, sit in front of dozens of beds. Feces and pools of urine dot the floor. In the midst of this excrement, 200 emaciated, sickly and deformed patients crawl on the floor, cry out in pain, yell Bengali phrases, bang empty water bottles, and scream incoherently. Pungent, disgusting odors and screeching, plaintive cries saturate the air.

I stand behind Sergio, to shield myself, and look up at him desperately for guidance. He strides resolutely into the huge chamber, removes two bedpans from the floor, and takes them to a dark, small concrete room where one of the Sisters of Charity, her blue and white outfit more grey and black in the dim light, cleans them with a hose and some rags. I put on a pair of plastic gloves and rush to help Sergio carry the heavy metal pans – carefully, lest the contents slosh onto the floor, or onto myself – into the dim and grimy room, and place them on a shelf where they wait for the sister to attend to them. It's disgusting, dirty work and it takes all of my willpower to keep myself from throwing up into a bedpan or onto the floor. What stops me is the thought that I'd have to clean it up.

Once we've removed the bedpans, Sergio begins to strip down the beds, but I'm gagging and trying not to cry and simply can't stay in this area any longer. I ask him to direct me to the laundry room. Once again, I have to do laundry because I can't stand to be near the patients. It's as if all my hard work counted for nothing – my ability to act decisively and compassionately has abandoned me, and I feel like the frightened little boy who first came to Calcutta. I cannot understand what happened to my strength, and the image of myself stirring clothes in the hot vat depresses me. This is not where I want to be. This is not why I came.

14.

The next day this routine repeats itself. I help remove the used bedpans from under the beds, after which I run to the sanctuary of the laundry room to gather my wits and catch my breath. After an hour or so, however, I head back into the patients' area.

The volunteers are now in the large outdoor courtyard, preparing to serve lunch. Having served in this capacity at Kalighat, I feel confident that this is something I can do.

Again, Prem Dam nearly overwhelms me. Volunteers place large metal vats of food on the table and nearly two hundred people surge forward. I suddenly find myself facing a courtyard full of screaming voices, cringing as hundreds of outstretched hands demand to be served first.

The seven of us hand out trays of food as fast as we can, trying to keep some semblance of order, hoping to keep the situation from degenerating into a riot. I have visions of desperate, starving people knocking us over, overturning the vats of food, and shoveling handfuls of rice and pieces of tandoori chicken into their mouths, but instead, as people get their food, the mob settles down, and finally, when everyone is eating, there's peace.

Once the able-bodied patients have their food, our next job is to take trays of food to those who cannot feed themselves. The German doctor who has taken it upon himself to organize the volunteers sends me to feed a gigantic young Indian man.

He is six foot three inches tall, about 18 years old and very handsome. Where most of the people here are bone thin, he is broad shouldered, heavyset and strong. As I approach him, he lies on the floor, completely, unnaturally, still. When I stand over him, tray in hand, his eyes move up to meet mine and he smiles. I realize that he's paralyzed from the neck down.

I sit down next to him and try to decide what to do. I need to find a way to prop up his gigantic head in order to feed him; but I also need to keep my hands free. It requires an intimacy that makes me uncomfortable, but I'll have to put his head in my lap. I put down the tray and lift up his head. Or I try to. It's only a head, but it's attached to his enormous, completely supine body. From my position sitting on the floor, it's very hard to lift all that dead weight. I manage to pick it up high enough for me to slide under him, and put his head down on my lap. But it's so heavy I'm not sure how I'll get up. It would be embarrassing to have to ask for help.

Once his head is in place, and I can start feeding him, I freeze up. For a moment, I really can't move, but the feeling vanishes when his big brown eyes search out my face, and his big mouth grins at me. He glows like a gigantic cherub, and I know that I can do this. As delicately as I can, I put spoonfuls of food into his mouth. He chews happily and smiles at me between bites like a big child. After he completes a mouthful, I ask him, "More?" And he smiles and opens his mouth. As he eats I have to wipe off his mouth and his cheeks, as food falls out of his mouth or off the spoon before it even gets to his mouth.

One of the reasons that food spills onto his face and the floor is that I'm wearing plastic gloves. Technically, I wear the gloves to protect myself from contracting diseases, but the truth is there's something very personal about skin on skin contact, and I'm afraid to get this close. But this boy deserves more than clumsy, insulated care, so I take off my gloves. I have a moment of fear as the spoon gets close to his mouth, and I worry that he may accidentally bite my hand, but the moment passes. I notice that he waits patiently for me to put the food on his tongue and doesn't begin chewing until he can see that the spoon is completely out of his mouth.

As I feed the young man, the German doctor passes by and slaps me on the back. "Great!" he shouts. "That's the spirit. Take off the gloves! How can you care for someone if you're afraid to touch him?"

When I come back the next day, the giant young man remembers me. He smiles at me and shakes his head to show me his joy. Now, there is at least one familiar face among the two hundred men I see here.

When I first arrived, the patients were a blur to me – anonymous and overwhelming conglomerations of suffering and pain – but as I learn about them, as I discover their personalities, they emerge from the crowd and gradually become individuals. Over time, as day passes day, their diseases and deformities vanish from my view until I no longer see them. Now, as it was at Kalighat, I only see people who care for me as I care for them.

Even the difficult or unpleasant residents become likeable once I get to know them. The most striking example of this occurs when I finally begin to understand one particular man. He is older than most of the people at the home. He has gray hair, is bone thin, and has a sharp, grating voice. He speaks no English, but manages to be bossy and authoritative just the same. After we remove the bedpans and wash the floor and the beds, we put clean bedpans under the patients' beds. Though the bedpans are of many shapes and sizes, most of the patients don't pay any attention to what they're given. But this man is different. When I approach his bed with a bedpan, he stands in my way, waiting to see what I've brought. Inevitably, he'll wave his hand at the bedpan and send me away with a disgusted shake of his head.

The room where we store the bedpans is the same room in which the sisters wash them. Not only does it smell awful, but there is something indescribably disturbing about being in a room where bedpans are cleaned daily, as if the taint of their uncleanliness has seeped into the floor, the walls, into the very air. It's repulsive to have to go into the room at all – I feel contaminated by it – and the idea that I have to repeatedly go into that room to please a bedpan connoisseur is torture. To make matters worse, his stringent ascetics do not limit themselves to bedpans alone. He is also an authority on piss bottles, water bottles and blankets. Each item is accepted only after he rejects the first few choices. After a few days of rushing to get him items that meet his specifications, I learn to either avoid him or simply force him to accept the first items I bring.

But, as I get to know the patients better, I begin to wonder if my judgment is misguided. What if he really has preferences about these items? To me they are all exactly the same, but it dawns on me that for this man they might be the only way he can express his personality. One day I bring all the different kinds of bedpans, piss bottles, and water bottles and let him choose, paying close attention to what he picks. The next day, I approach him with the same items and wait to see if he'll reject them. Instead, he's so happy that I know what he wants he does a little dance.

As the days go on, I find myself moving into a sacred space. Whatever I'm doing becomes the most important thing I have ever done. When I bring someone a glass of water, his eyes glow with gratitude. When I come to someone's assistance, his body softens and his face relaxes, smiling up at me with love. When someone is dying, every moment, every action, can become precious. Again, I'm learning to be present to the needs of others and to my actions and feelings, without thought or judgment or fear, and in doing so each moment is transformed. I experience my every action as essential, holy; and it energizes me. I go home each day riding a euphoric high, happy with myself and my day.

I feel so good, in fact, that I feel guilty. My image of service is that it should be enervating, exhausting work. It should feel like sacrifice. I worry that my enjoyment means I'm still a selfish person at heart. Then I remember that Mother Theresa once said, "the people I serve give me so much more than I give them." At the time, I thought it was something a saint was supposed to say, something that no one was really meant to believe. But, I realize now that I was wrong. The love I receive from the patients far outweighs my efforts. Mother Theresa spoke the plain truth after all, and I understand her hidden message. If giving feels like sacrifice it's because it's done resentfully, because the giver wants something in return, be it money or gratitude or respect. The feeling of sacrifice occurs because the giver doesn't feel like the return is worth the investment he makes. A true act of love, however, where the giver expects and desires nothing in return, fills the giver with joy and contentment, for the action itself is its own reward. It's a full circle, where everyone benefits.

It's incredible to discover that I can live this way. That I *can* serve and love. That a life of helping others can be more enriching and joyous than anything I've experienced before.

15.

One of the most special aspects of my work at Prem Dam comes upon me unexpectedly. Most of the patients are able to wash themselves, but there are a few people who are so sick or are in so much pain that they can't even get out of bed. A tall German man named Franz has been helping two of these people since I arrived, but when we get a new bedridden patient he decides that he needs some help. David, the German doctor, gathers our small group of volunteers together and asks for someone to assist this man.

My friend Miri washed patients on the women's side at Kalighat, and I remember her describing the work. "The human touch is so important," she told me. "No one thinks much about my work as a hairdresser, but it's actually very intimate work. I wash the women's hair with warm water, I massage the scalp with the shampoo, and they sit back and relax as I cut their hair. They tell me of their boyfriends, their dreams, their disappointments. I listen and cut and shape and dry, but all the while we share something very intimate. Outside of my shop, we may be strangers, but when they come to me we are close confidants. Washing these patients is very similar. Many of these women have never been touched by anyone but their husbands since they have become adults, and many of their husbands don't touch them with kindness. When I wash them, they sigh and smile. It's like they didn't know they could be loved."

When I listened to her, I felt envy and also pain: envy that she was experiencing something so special and pain that I could not bring myself to help the men at Kalighat in this way.

But I am no longer that person. I have changed. I raise my hand and volunteer.

First thing the next morning, after we collect the bedpans and dirty laundry, Franz and I carry three beds from the dorm room into one of the side entrances. An old man, all elbows and knees and bony protrusions, lies in the first bed. He looks up at me with big frightened eyes when we pick up his bed, moans in pain, and reaches up in supplication as if he thinks I am an angel of death come to take him away. I smile at him, hoping to reassure him, but he moans and lies back in bed.

A middle-aged man, his face pale as chalk, lies in the second bed. He grunts softly when we pick up his bed but after that – even though he clenches his teeth in agony – he makes no noise at all.

A young boy, in his early twenties, his face unlined and apparently innocent, lies in the third bed. He screams when we pick up the bed and moans and pleads all the way to the washing room. When we gently set down the bed, he turns his head to the side and cries softly.

Because they spend all day in their little beds and do not have the strength to use a bedpan, urine and feces saturate their sheets. To prevent the spread of disease and infection, they must endure the daily pain and humiliation of being cleaned and moved by us. Without equipment or training, we don't know how to support their fragile bodies as we move them from one bed to another. Franz lifts them up by their shoulders, I grab their legs and as smoothly and gently as we can, we move them from the dirty bed onto a clean one. Despite our best efforts, the movements agonize all our patients as our operation is fairly clumsy.

Once we place them on a clean bed, we undress them and sponge them down with water. It's an awkward process. None of them can stand, so we have to roll them to one side, undress and wash half of their bodies, and then roll them the other way to complete the task. And this must be done with the utmost care. The old man has large red scrapes and sores all over his body. The middle-aged man has a large white hole in his backside, which I'm told is cancer. It stinks like death, and he convulses in agony when we clean it. The young boy is a bit of a mystery. Though he screams and shouts with every touch, his body reveals no obvious wounds.

Every morning, for an hour and a half, Franz and I minister to these three dying men. He doesn't speak English and I don't know German, so we communicate through tone of voice and body language. Within a few days we fall into a rhythmic, quiet working relationship. Due to the nature of the work, the need for extreme care at all times, I find that I'm aware of every action I make, every motion that Franz makes, and every sound or movement that the patients make. Something special happens in this space. Light seems to cling to our bodies, as if our daily washing somehow transcends mechanical functions and transmutes love and care into something palpable.

The intensity of this work concentrates my mind. I have the experience of being present to every moment and every action, and this focused awareness transforms time into something translucent and precious. The experience I had with the dying English teacher in Kalighat is magnified here, extended, so that I know it is possible to live every moment in this way. Forgetting about the past, not worrying about the future, and not judging the present, but simply experiencing and being aware of what is actually happening turns these simple actions, these moments of washing and moving and touching, into holy, sacred life.

Over the next two weeks, the two older men die. They both bore their illnesses and suffering with dignity, but I think that death must be a welcome release for them. I never learn their names, but I feel their absence. Prem Dam feels slightly empty and hollow once they are gone. But the emptiness, I know, is really in me.

16.

When the French soldiers learn about the lack of help at Prem Dam, my routine is abruptly altered. Where before I had been busy from the moment I stepped into the center to the moment I left, I again find myself without anything to do. Everywhere I go, people are doing the jobs that I had seemed to own. The amazing feeling of being needed, of my every action having deep meaning, is gone. Even the giant quadriplegic, who I had fed every day, has a new helper. And now he smiles at him! At the end of the day I'm frustrated and angry. How dare these new people come here and take my work from me?

As I sit in my hotel room, sulking, I hear my self-righteous internal voice, and it shocks me. How did my desire to serve selflessly become so selfish?

I remember when I was at Kalighat, people often asked for cookies or a massage and I felt sorry I couldn't comply. Wouldn't it be nice, I thought then, if I had time to sit with them and get to know them, rather than simply rushing to fill immediate, desperate needs? Now that I had a chance to do that, I spent it brooding angrily. I feel like a fool.

On the other hand, I remind myself, knowing I was foolish today gives me a chance to do something different tomorrow.

The next morning I spend time with some of the people I have come to know. I bring them blankets and water. I hand out biscuits. I sit beside them and enjoy the sun and their company. And when someone asks for a massage, I smile, nod, and walk into the volunteer room to retrieve the bottle of skin cream.

The moment I step out into the courtyard with the bottle in my hand, people rush towards me. Before I know it, a very patient, un-Indian like line has formed. Suddenly, I'm not sure this was a good idea. I've never given a massage before. But I decide that, perhaps, skill is not essential here. I remember Father O'Toole's speech about the Untouchables being literally untouchable, and I remember the leper colony, where being touched was such an important part of their happiness. Perhaps the simple touch of someone gentle, someone who cares, is what is required. Besides, I reason, free help is hard to find. And they don't speak English, so it's not as though they can complain.

Although I've never done this before, I quickly find a groove. Each patient indicates a body part – his arm, leg, or back for me to massage – and I spend about 5 minutes rubbing the cream into the dried, tight muscles. As I work, I focus on how their muscles feel, searching for the right amount of pressure to apply – enough so I can have an effect, without being so forceful that I hurt them.

I enjoy this, until I notice a certain man at the end of the line. Of all the residents here, this man is the most ugly. He has a gigantic head, which is accentuated by his very narrow shoulders, a big bulbous nose and a bulky clubfoot. Since he can't use either leg very well, he has to drag his deformed body across the ground with the strength of his spindly arms. He often defecates on the ground, and sits helplessly next to it, crying out for someone to come and clean it up. Though I pity him, I can't stand to see or be around him. I have so completely avoided him that I have even forgotten he lives here. But now, there he is, at the end of my massage line, patiently waiting his turn.

Despite his looming presence, I manage to focus on each patient as he sits in front of me. My gentle touch and the soothing power of the cream to moisten dry, cracked skin creates a bond between us, and I try to focus on this connection. But, between patients, my mind returns to the problem at hand. How can I get away from that disgusting man?

The massage line gets shorter and shorter until, finally, he's the only one left.

He slides his broken body over the ground and holds out his legs. Naturally, it would be his legs. They're disgusting. The dark brown skin is scaly, cracked, and has a white powdery sheen to it. And the left leg has that horribly misshapen, enormous, clubfoot, about half again as wide as his foot should be.

I point to his arms and his back, but he shakes his gigantic head slowly back and forth and stubbornly holds out his good leg. It looks unpleasant to touch and I consider refusing, telling him that I'm sorry, I have to go, or at least returning to the volunteer office to pick up a pair of rubber gloves, but this strange, ugly man sits before me, insistent, and patient. I see no way out. I hold my breath, put lotion on my hands, and begin.

At first the hideous skin feels like leather, but it softens, and the scales dissolve when the cream is rubbed in. The leg slowly transforms into a normal texture and sheen. Maybe, I think, I can get away with only doing the one leg.

When I finish massaging his good foot, I quickly turn to gather my things, hoping I can get up before he can react, but it's a foolish, desperate thought. The leg with the clubfoot is in front of me. There's no way I can spurn him without being insulting and rude, and I can't bring myself to do this.

Again, the magic transformation begins as I rub the moisturizer into his scaly skin. As I work, I can feel his gaze upon me. When I look up, he is staring intently at me, watching me. I don't know why. Then, our eyes locked together, he touches his forehead with his hand and touches my feet.

Most Indian women wear a red marker, called a bindi, between their eyes, to symbolize the belief that there exists a form of higher consciousness, where the energy flow of the body is reversed and a mystical "third" eye emerges. This is the spot the man touches, and when his hand touches my feet, I'm aware of energy coursing through my body. It feels very intimate, and it makes me uncomfortable.

"Don't do that," I say as I massage his thigh, his knee. Again, he touches his forehead and touches my feet. Again I feel flushed. "Don't do that." I say, strongly this time. When I get to his calf, he does it a third time and I feel lightheaded, embarrassed and somehow vulnerable.

I touch my forehead and then touch his foot, as if I can send this energy back, but he instantly returns the gesture. I try to stop his hand, but he eludes me.

We do this a few times – he blesses me, I return it, and quick as a flash, he's touched his forehead and touched my feet again. After a few of these exchanges, I give up and accept his gestures.

I massage his leg until, to my horror, I've reached the moment I've been dreading. His clubfoot is before me, the only part of his legs left to massage. I hold my breath and gingerly touch it. It feels....like skin. No different. No worse.

I slowly massage it, relieved to discover that although it looks ugly, it's just muscle and human skin. Again and again he touches his forehead and touches my feet, and I begin to feel giddy, energetic, high on something.

At the mission, there were quotations from Jesus exhorting his followers to treat other human beings as they would treat him. "Whatsoever you do to the least of my brothers, you do unto me." This is not meant as mere allegory, but intended as a literal truth. Every human being is believed to have been created in the image of God, to have, in fact, the divine spark of God within him. The goal of our clothing, feeding, touching, and caring for the Untouchables is to learn to treat each person, even the lowest, most deformed, diseased or demented as if he were the Lord himself. This is the sacred mission. We are not ministering to strangers, but to incarnations of God himself.

Hindu believers see their gurus in much the same manner. These saintly men and women are, at a minimum, a vehicle for one to communicate with

God. But for many, the guru is actually a divine incarnation of God himself. To touch the guru is to touch the living form of God, and disciples often receive divine blessings by touching the guru's holy feet.

As I massage this man's foot, I am conscious of these beliefs coming together. I am treating this man as if he were God, serving him as if his body was the body of a holy saint or an enlightened guru. I could not be more gentle or caring if my own mother were before me, and this is God's secret, blessed gift. To treat a human being as an image of the beloved, as an incarnation of the divine, is to unveil God's essential nature in man. I am not massaging the club foot of a stranger, but the broken body of God itself.

In return he worships me as his guru, submitting to my ministering touch by passing energy to me. We're enveloped in an unbroken circuit of care where I gently comfort him and he graces me with gratitude.

The artificial boundaries between us vanish. His physical ugliness disappears. My superior status fades away. We are simply two human beings, reveling in the reality of this eternal and dynamic moment. I feel the warmth of his flesh, the glow of the sunlight which envelops us, the tactile presence of our mutual love. Only this moment exists, and everything exists in this moment. Our imperfections are unveiled as essential components of our unadorned inner beauty. When a person gives of himself with an open heart, expecting nothing in return, and when another receives this gift with unfettered gratitude, feeling no debt, love is invoked as a palpable force, uniting and binding us together. Illusions of the self disappear, and our divine nature is revealed.

I remain locked in the moment's embrace until the pale, rough, scaly skin of his clubfoot is soft, supple and brown. I remove my hands from his flesh. He bows before me and drags himself away. I stand up and discover that I can't feel the ground beneath my feet, and I can hardly see my surroundings at all. Everything is bright and hazy. I feel dizzy and lightheaded, unable to transition back into my normal perception of reality.

I stand uncertainly in the courtyard, amazed. The idea that God created man in his image is no mere allegory. It is real, and for an uncertain moment, I witnessed and was a part of this truth. I saw God incarnate. I reached out to him and massaged his mangled foot. And in doing so, God blessed me.

Afterward

I wish that was the end of the story. In the Hollywood movie version, the person who had that experience would have finished his journey, understood everything he needed to understand, and lived happily ever after. But the truth wasn't like that. That massage was an amazing experience, but it didn't mark the end of my journey.

I continued to travel around India until my visa ran out, before going to Nepal. I had determined not to return home until I knew what I wanted to do with my life, and even after Calcutta, I didn't have that insight. Despite the fact that my sense of joy had vanished, and I could feel that there was nothing left for me to do, I stubbornly refused to listen. When my father was diagnosed with cancer, however, I had to return home. Soon afterwards, my brother was also diagnosed with cancer. My mother and I did our best to support them, and I was very grateful for my experiences in Calcutta, because I understood how important my mere presence at this time really was. Fortunately, both my father and brother recovered, and both are healthy now.

I lived in Montana for two years, and then Israel, also for two years. Each time, I followed the call of my inner voice. I didn't know why I wanted to move to these places, but when I thought about going, I felt that inexplicable feeling of joy which told me that I did, in fact, want to go. In each location I had experiences which helped me discover more of my hidden virtues, gain increased confidence in myself, and feel happier and healthier. And each experience somehow led to the next. It was as if I had an experience in order to unlock some potential in myself, and once this was revealed, I was ready to tackle the next task. Each journey improved my self-knowledge, from thinking I wanted to be a writer, a teacher, a rabbi, until I finally understood myself well enough to know that the most natural fit of my interests and talents could be found in the work of being a mental health counselor. I love listening to people's stories. I love helping people. I passionately believe in people's ability to grow and to find happiness, and the idea that I could help others do this excited me.

I moved back to New York, studied social work, and afterwards received training in psychoanalysis. It's amazing. I never encountered a more fulfilling or exciting job. Even though the trip to India in and of itself did not reveal to me my career path, the practice of following my inner voice slowly led me to it. That inner voice also led me to the sense of security and peace I needed to be ready to find my wife. Fifteen years after my trip to India, I am in love, I'm married and I have a career. I also have a son. I feel very very fortunate.

Throughout the years, I have learned to better appreciate the unique, intelligent and loving person I can be. I have continued my meditation practice which helps me understand myself and heal. I try to listen to my heart and follow my inner sense of joy where it leads me. And most importantly, I understand my spiritual path.

During my travels, I had an opportunity to experience the beauty and wisdom of different ancient traditions, and I truly believe that they provide people who are sincere in their desire to get closer to God with tools and practices to help make this possible. But God is greater than any tradition. To say that God can only be reached or understood in one way is to define, demarcate, demean and diminish God. As God is infinite, so there are infinite paths one can take to get closer to God.

My path, I have begun to understand, is the path of love. It is what has guided my journey, and it is what I try to use to focus my thoughts and actions. It has been said that God is love itself. What I know is that the more I follow my joy, the more I listen to my heart, the healthier and happier I become. And God's true secret seems to be that healthy, happy people naturally spread joy and love to others. Love is contagious. The more I love myself, the more I see in others that is worthy of love. The more I love myself and others, the more I love life itself – and God cannot be separated from life, they are indivisible. I know that whatever I do in the future, my journey will be a blessing to those I encounter along the way and to myself. I'm excited to follow my joy and can only marvel and wonder where it will lead me next.

I sincerely hope that this book has helped inspire you to do the same.

Acknowledgements

I am indebted to many people who helped me turn events from my life into a written memoir. First and foremost, I want to thank my wife. She has been patient, reading many versions of the stories in this book, kind with her feedback, and supportive of the idea that I had an experience worth sharing. She is beautiful, compassionate, strong and wise. I am blessed to have her in my life. This story in some ways is a description of how I became the man who could capture her heart. I want her to know that having her in my life makes everything better. I am grateful for the family we're creating, and I will do what I can to ensure I am worthy of her love.

Second, I want to thank my brother Randy. He was encouraging and supportive of my writing, even when it was raw and not done well. He read many versions of these stories, and provided his honest feedback about what was inspiring, what was funny, what was gross, and what simply was not working. I was grateful to have his companionship when we were growing up, and I'm proud to think I played a role in his becoming the intelligent, wise, strong, and caring man he is today.

Third, I want to thank Michael Kaye. Not only are you an extraordinary writer and editor, but you are a funny and caring friend. Your professional feedback, over the two versions of the book you edited, helped me find my storyline and refine my writing voice. This book would not be as good as it is without your help.

In addition to the three people mentioned above, I was fortunate to have the help and support of friends and family who read versions of this book and provided their feedback, support, and assistance: Carol &

Michael Kurtz, Rena & Alan Steinfeld, Lauren Kurtz, Jeff Kutash, Amir Monsefi, Dave Weinstein, Judy & Rob Stern, Roberta Danza, Harvey Krueger, Ike Sorkin, Larry Seeman, Jacqueline Stolte, Karen Shaw-Coletta, Terry Zuckerman, Josh Olesker, Charles Thomas, Christine Grounds, Lee Kramer, Kathleen Quinn, Carol Guber, John McCaffrey, Kevin Burke, Amy Lieberman, Nancy Bravman, Sharilyn Cohn, Barb Cabot, Sandy & Harry LaForge, Lynn Redding, Tony Pederson, Mikael Romano, Elizabeth Brown, Ezra Shapiro, Rev. Yakov Nagen, and Elad Zlotnick. Thank you for believing in me enough to read this when it was raw and for your support and encouragement throughout this process.

When I think about my life and all the amazing people who are and have been in it, it's sometimes hard to believe it's all real. Thank you for helping me create a community where I feel appreciated, and where I can love and grow.

About the Author

Jason Kurtz has been a production assistant for Writer's Cinema, a bit actor in the short film Brain Drain, an entry level employee for a PR company, a marketing coordinator for Technics Musical Instruments, the registrar for The Chalice of Repose Project, an assistant to the Communications Director for the Missoula Demonstration Project, an English as a Foreign Language teacher, and a Mental Health Counselor at the Union Settlement Association. He has studied Spanish in Guatemala and Costa Rica, Hebrew at WUJUS, Judaism at Yeshivat Otniel in Israel, and Psychoanalysis at the Training Institute for Mental Health. He holds a Master's Degree in English Literature and one in Social Work from New York University, and a BA in English Literature from Brandeis University. He is currently in private practice as a psychotherapist in Manhattan, and is the Director of Training at the Training Institute for Mental Health. He is happily married to the woman of his dreams, and is the proud father of Asher Jacob Kurtz.

Made in the USA
Las Vegas, NV
13 December 2021

37499805R10162